TRUCKING REGULATION

AEI-Hoover
policy studies

The studies in this series are issued jointly
by the American Enterprise Institute
for Public Policy Research and the Hoover
Institution on War, Revolution and Peace.
They are designed to focus on
policy problems of current and future interest,
to set forth the factors underlying
these problems and to evaluate
courses of action available to policy makers.
The views expressed in these studies
are those of the authors and do not necessarily
reflect the views of the staff, officers
or members of the governing boards of
AEI or the Hoover Institution.

TRUCKING REGULATION

Lessons from Europe

Thomas Gale Moore

American Enterprise Institute for Public Policy Research
Washington, D. C.

Hoover Institution on War, Revolution and Peace
Stanford University, Stanford, California

AEI-Hoover Policy Study 18, January 1976
(Hoover Institution Studies 54)

ISBN 0-8447-3188-9
Library of Congress Catalog Card No. 75-42811

Printed in United States of America

Contents

List of Tables

WEST GERMANY

BELGIUM

NETHERLANDS

SWEDEN

Preface

This study resulted from countless interviews in the five countries studied—Great Britain, West Germany, Belgium, the Netherlands, and Sweden. Government officials and representatives of trade associations, shippers, shipper associations, and truckers were interviewed. The identity of particular companies has been kept confidential.

I would like to thank all involved, although they are too numerous to name here. Brian Bayliss in England, James M. Pascall in West Germany, Lars Kritz in Sweden, and Louis Eeckhoudt in Belgium were especially helpful. Spokesmen for shippers and truckers also contributed greatly to this study but for reasons of confidentiality cannot be named here. I would also like to thank James Miller III and Yale Brozen for carefully reading the manuscript and making many valuable suggestions. Errors in the work and in the interpretation of the data are solely the responsibility of the author.

Finally I would like to thank my wife, Cassandra, and my children, Charles and Antonia, for their patience during my long absences collecting data. I should like also to thank the Smith Richardson Foundation, Inc., the American Enterprise Institute, and the Hoover Institution on War, Revolution and Peace for supporting this study.

Introduction

Starting in the 1960s the attitudes of government officials, academic experts, and media personnel towards regulation of the transportation industries have radically changed. For example, in 1962 President Kennedy proposed the elimination of minimum rate control of freight transportation.[1] The 1964 Report of the Hilton Task Forces on National Transportation Policy, which was drafted mainly by academic economists, recommended placing greater reliance on market forces and less on public regulation.[2] In 1971 the Department of Transportation proposed reducing entry barriers for professional trucking and removing many restrictions on existing carriers.[3] None of these proposals has met with success in the Congress.

Trucking industry spokesmen have been generally opposed to changes of this sort. They have claimed that without regulation "cut-throat competition" would prevail and there would be chaos.[4] Congress has also been told that regulation preserves profits and therefore encourages firms to provide better service and gives them sufficient margin to enable them to serve small towns and remote areas. Without regulation, it has been argued, small towns and remote areas are bound to suffer.

Economists and other scholars (this author included) have testified that regulation is unnecessary to preserve stability and enhance quality of service—that in a free market the quality of service would depend

---

[1] U.S., Congress, House, *Transportation Message of 1962*, 87th Cong., 2d sess., 1962, House document no. 384.

[2] "Report to the President of the United States," November 1964.

[3] Transportation Regulatory Modernization Act of 1971, S. 2842.

[4] *Transportation . . . Regulation or Disaster?* (Washington, D. C.: American Trucking Association, n.d.), p. 8.

on customer needs and desires, that it would certainly not necessarily be worse than it is now and would probably be better in remote areas, and that regulation has fostered both monopoly and costly inefficiency. These scholars have been accused of being theorists out of touch with the real world.

Fortunately European experience can provide a test of the effects of regulation on the motor carrier industry and on shippers as well. Some European countries have virtually no economic regulation of transportation, while in others, transportation is almost as controlled as the interstate trucking industry in the United States. Moreover, three European countries have deregulated or partially deregulated truck transportation in the period following World War II. We can therefore look at their experience with the transitional problem of moving from a tightly controlled system to a more liberal one.

The primary objective of this study is to use European experience to measure the impact of regulation on the trucking industry (and therefore on the railroads) and on shippers. The study is fundamentally an effort to measure the consequences of economic regulation empirically. Government and industry data were collected in each country. In most cases officials and industry spokesmen were most helpful.

Besides attempting to measure the impact of regulation on the trucking industry, this study seeks to throw light on the interaction of political and economic behavior. It is my belief that some general conclusions about the relationship of regulation to industry behavior can be drawn from the data presented here. Even though this is a study of the trucking industry, the conclusions may be equally valid for other regulated industries. At least what has been done here should illustrate the main forces behind the establishment of regulation of an industry and the way regulation works out in practice. Even though specific details differ among industries, regulation can be expected to have similar results for all inherently competitive industries such as trucking and transportation generally.

Five countries—Great Britain, West Germany, Belgium, the Netherlands, and Sweden—were chosen for study. Since international traffic is important on the continent, and especially so for Belgium and the Netherlands, I also made a brief study of Common Market transport policy. Great Britain was chosen because the road haulage industry was almost completely deregulated by a 1968 act of Parliament, the only remaining controls being those designed to improve safety on the high-

2

ways (rather as though, for our air transport, the CAB were eliminated with the FAA remaining). West Germany was included because it has the most strictly controlled long-distance trucking industry on the continent, both entry and rates being regulated by the federal government. Belgium deregulated its professional trucking industry substantially in 1960 and entry is relatively easy. From 1962 on, Sweden has taken steps towards a major reduction in entry barriers for road haulage firms. The Netherlands was included partly because it is a mixed case—with entry fairly easy in some sectors of the industry and difficult if not impossible in others—and partly because the Dutch are known as the most efficient truckers in Western Europe and dominate the international haulage market there.

In each of these countries, I visited the government departments responsible for transportation and any regulatory bodies involved. I interviewed the major national road haulage associations, as well as trade associations representing own-account shippers and users of professional carriers. I consulted transport research institutes and academic scholars of transportation, and I questioned a few large shippers: one that used truckers in all the countries was extremely helpful. I visited at least one professional road haulage firm in each country, and these firms turned out to be helpful also. In fact, they often produced insights into the workings of the industry that I would not have gained from discussions with government personnel. For example, government policies were sometimes being circumvented either without the knowledge of officials or at least without their acknowledgment. These visits, interviews, and discussions produced a vast amount of data, only a small portion of which is included in this study.

In several ways my own views have been modified by what I found out. It is apparent that there are some economies of scale in the trucking industry with the smallest firms, those with one truck, having higher costs than larger-sized firms. It is also apparent that with or without regulatory restraints most firms will specialize by area served and often by product carried. As a result only a handful of firms are ever in direct competition, but potential competition can restrain even the most oligopolistic-appearing situation. Most firms build long-term connections with their customers, even though formal contracts are unusual. Thus the casual "day market" subject to price cutting on the part of new firms or truckers looking for a back haul tends to be generally unimportant.

3

A surprising factor, at least to me, was how important national characteristics seem to have been in determining industry behavior. It sounds like a stereotype but it is true that the English do "muddle through" while the Germans organize everything. Admittedly, competitive pressures (or the absence of competitive pressures) may modify these national characteristics, but they do not change their fundamental pattern. For example, one Belgian trucker told me how one of his drivers went with a tractor to meet a trailer sent by an English trucking firm by channel ferry. The British firm did not deliver the trailer to the ferry and forgot to notify him that it would not be arriving.

Of course, other factors also lead to significant differences among countries. The heavy taxes levied in Sweden and in the Netherlands produce many illegal unlicensed firms, even though entry restrictions in Sweden at least have been minimal in recent years. Geographical differences among the countries, which are substantial, have a major impact on the freight business. Sweden is large but sparsely populated, the Netherlands small and very densely populated. In England population and industry are concentrated in London and the Midlands, while in Germany there is no single urban center comparable to London and industry is spread relatively evenly throughout the country.

Transportation infrastructure likewise has a major impact on transport industries. In Holland and Belgium inland waterways are of major importance for bulk commodities. In Sweden the road network does not reach all northern points and rail transport does. In Great Britain there are comparatively few miles of limited-access four-lane highways and most roads are two-lane, twisty, and slow. In Germany, on the other hand, a reasonably complete network of autobahns links all major cities.

It cannot be overemphasized that there is no demand for "transportation" but rather a multitude of demands for the transportation of specific commodities between specific points under specific conditions. Each of these demands has produced special carriers designed to serve the special demand. To the extent that shipper needs differ among countries, industry characteristics also differ.

Notwithstanding these caveats, it has been possible to come to some conclusions about the impact of regulation, its objectives, and its origins. A careful analysis shows striking differences in industry performance that can only be the result of the presence or absence of regulatory constraints. Strict regulation leads to higher rates, poorer

4

service, and a decline in efficiency. The outcome of deregulation is quite apparent in Great Britain and Sweden. Deregulation, while resulting in lower rates, does not lead to cut-throat competition or instability.

In each of the chapters describing the individual countries, the regulatory system is described and there is a short historical section on the origins of trucking regulation and any substantial changes that have been made in regulation. After this descriptive material has been presented, the effects of the country's regulatory system are analyzed.

The next chapter is devoted to overall comparisons and conclusions. Here, as we contrast similar transport systems, differing essentially in regulatory constraints, the effects of regulation become apparent. From the comparison it is possible to draw some striking conclusions about the general impact of regulation even though specific elements of the regulatory systems differ sharply.

Lessons for the United States are drawn in the final chapter, which outlines the regulatory system in the United States, its origins, and its effects. An attempt is made to compare and contrast U.S. regulation with regulation found in Europe.

1
Regulation of Trucking in Great Britain

Since 1 December 1970 there has been no effective control over entry into any branch of the British trucking industry. There has never been any control over rates except in conjunction with economy-wide price controls designed to control inflation. As a consequence, except for vehicle safety regulations and driver hours limitations, trucking in Great Britain is completely free of government control.

The 1968 Transport Act established the basic ground rules under which the industry now operates. This act was designed to substitute "quality" regulation for "quantity" regulation. It eliminated the need for the operator of any vehicle under three and a half tons gross weight to secure any permit except for a normal vehicle license and a general driver's license for the operator.[1] Operators of these vehicles are obliged by law to meet the vehicle maintenance requirements and the drivers' hours requirements specified in the 1968 act, but they do not need to keep records to prove compliance.

Operators of larger vehicles, whether for-hire or own-account— that is, private trucking—are required to secure an Operator's License ("O" license) from the licensing authority of the area in which the person wishes to have an operating center.[2] If a firm or person wishes to operate from more than one area, an "O" license must be secured from each of the licensing authorities in whose territory a terminal is desired.[3] Once a person has secured an "O" license, he is free to carry any goods, to any place, at any rate, for any shipper, but he has no common-carrier

---

[1] Great Britain, Transport Act, 1968, pt. 5, par. 60.
[2] Ibid.
[3] Ibid., par. 62.

7

obligations. No distinction is made between private and for-hire operators.

The requirements to secure an "O" license are that

(1) the applicant be a fit person,

(2) satisfactory arrangements have been made to ensure that the provision of the act dealing with drivers' hours will be met, and

(3) there will be satisfactory facilities and arrangements for maintaining the authorized vehicles in a fit and serviceable condition.[4]

The licensing authority is authorized at its discretion to investigate whether the applicant has sufficient financial resources to meet requirement (3) above. If the applicant meets all three requirements, the licensing authority must grant the "O" license.[5]

When an application for an "O" license is received, the licensing authority must publish the fact in a statement called "Applications and Decisions." Specified trade unions, the two main haulage associations, the police, or local authorities may object to the granting of the "O" license on the grounds that one or more of the conditions, (1) through (3), is not or will not be met.[6] Should an objection be made or should the licensing authority consider a hearing necessary, a public hearing may be held. If the application is denied or an objection overruled, the "injured party" may appeal to the Transport Tribunal.

The law provided for the introduction of a transport manager's licensing system and a "quantity" licensing system for the largest lorries when used for hauls of over 100 miles. The first provision was repealed, while the second has never been put into effect, although it does remain on the statute books.[7] The Conservative government under Edward Heath said that it would never be put into effect, and the new Labour government under Harold Wilson has not expressed itself on the subject. Before the February 1974 election, the Labour party had pledged to nationalize much of the road haulage industry, but no action has been taken.

The transition from the old licensing system to the new "quality" licensing took several years. In 1969, after passage of the Transport Act, all constraints on vehicles under three and a half tons were removed. The operators' licensing system for larger vehicles did not begin to be

---

4 Ibid., par. 64.

5 Ibid.

6 Ibid., par. 63.

7 Ibid., par. 71.

put into effect until March 1970 and it was not until 1 December 1970, that the operators' licensing system was extended to vehicles larger than five tons unladen weight used for journeys of over 100 miles. The transition was not complete until the end of the first quarter of 1971.

Industry spokesmen have asserted that the right to object to an application for a new license does not prevent "fly-by-night" operators from entering the industry.[8] Often a licensing authority must simply rely on the promises of a new applicant to meet the drivers' hours and maintenance requirements. Only with experience is the licensing authority in a position to establish whether a person will in fact meet the requirements.

Tables GB–1 and GB–2 make it clear that entry is virtually free. In the year ending 30 September 1972, there were 15,956 "new" applications, of which 14,818 (or 93 percent) were approved and only 473 (or about 3 percent) denied. The total number of objections lodged during that year was eleven: three from the police (with one each in the northwestern, eastern and Scottish traffic areas), three from local authorities (all in the southeastern traffic area), and five from the Road Haulage Association (three in the northern and two in the east Midland traffic areas). It has been claimed with some apparent validity that the objection procedure is worthless, and the industry would certainly like to see it made easier to object and to have an objection sustained, although there is no real pressure to go back to "quantity" licensing.[9]

Historical Background

The Road and Rail Traffic Act of 1933 established the regulatory system that, with modifications, remained intact until the passage of the 1968 act. Railroad rates had been based on the principle of charging what the traffic would bear. With the development of the motor vehicle and consequent truck-rail competition, the railroads—burdened with discriminatory rate structures—found it increasingly difficult to compete. As a result their most valuable traffic drifted to road haulage and they were left with the low-value, low-profit traffic. As the depression of the 1930s deepened, bankruptcies became more common generally, al-

---

[8] Interview with Eric W. Russel, secretary of the Road Haulage Association, 5 October 1973.
[9] Ibid.

Table GB-1

NUMBER OF APPLICATIONS FOR OPERATORS' LICENSES, BY TRAFFIC AREA, FOR THE YEAR ENDING 30 SEPTEMBER 1972

| Traffic Area | Applications outstanding at end of previous year | New and Regrant Licenses | | Applications refused | Interim Licenses Issued | Cases Heard at Public Inquiry (arising from all applications) |
		Applications received	Licenses issued			
Northern	153 (151)	1,274 (885)	1,029 (771)	16 (13)	521	171
Yorkshire	96 (95)	2,268 (1,539)	1,653 (1,177)	24 (24)	545	179
Northwestern	545 (528)	3,378 (2,404)	2,805 (2,145)	75 (66)	1,184	272
West Midland	272 (272)	2,739 (1,783)	2,257 (1,612)	95 (88)	171	221
East Midland	167 (151)	2,086 (1,396)	1,770 (1,194)	53 (44)	1,211	238
Eastern	425 (414)	1,673 (1,183)	1,452 (1,089)	32 (31)	653	291
South Wales	250 (250)	1,156 (760)	949 (675)	58 (50)	482	827
Western	516 (221)	1,976 (812)	1,809 (736)	76 (60)	190	242
Southeastern	420 (390)	1,638 (1,480)	1,655 (1,514)	48 (44)	225	97
Metropolitan	1,028 (968)	3,571 (2,533)	3,326 (2,786)	3 (3)	592	412
Scottish	358 (344)	1,813 (1,181)	1,511 (1,119)	54 (50)	599	418
Total	4,230 (3,784)	23,569 (15,956)	20,216 (14,818)	534 (473)	6,373	3,368

Note: Figures in parentheses refer to new applications only.

Source: Department of the Environment, "Annual Reports of the Licensing Authorities, 1971–1972," mimeographed (London, 1973).

Table GB–2

NUMBER OF OPERATORS HOLDING "O" LICENSES AND NUMBER OF "O" LICENSED VEHICLES, BY TRAFFIC AREA, FOR THE YEAR ENDING 30 SEPTEMBER 1972

Traffic Area	Number of Operators	Number of Vehicles		
		Tractive units	Rigid	Total
Northern	7,314	5,448	23,887	29,335
Yorkshire	12,267	8,050	39,527	47,577
Northwestern	18,650	15,442	60,112	75,554
West Midland	14,639	9,987	45,119	55,106
East Midland	11,664	8,907	37,292	46,199
Eastern	8,758	6,623	24,963	31,586
South Wales	5,353	3,553	17,003	20,556
Western	10,006	6,015	33,773	39,788
Southeastern	9,187	5,516	32,482	37,998
Metropolitan	20,180	15,609	75,592	91,201
Scottish	12,472	8,725	40,384	49,109
Total	130,490	93,875	430,134	524,009

Note: Operators with operating centers in more than one traffic area hold separate operators' licenses in each traffic area as required by section 61(2) of the Transport Act 1968. Consequently the figure given in the first column is greater than the total number of licensed operators in the country.

Source: Department of the Environment, "Annual Reports of the Licensing Authorities, 1971–1972."

though work done by Professors MacLeod and Walters suggests that the bankruptcy rate among truckers was lower than it was in some other trades that consisted largely of small firms.[10] Two British government reports in the early 1930s recommended regulation, partly to establish "fair wages" and improved vehicle maintenance, but mostly to avoid the "evils of excessive competition." No evidence was offered that there was "excessive competition."

The 1933 act provided for three kinds of licenses: The "A" license for professional carriers, the "B" license for own-account operators who wished to carry for other people as well, and the "C" license for those own-account operators carrying only for themselves. In addition the act provided for the "A" contract license which permitted a firm to

[10] W. M. MacLeod and A. A. Walters, "A Note on Bankruptcy in Road Haulage," *Journal of Industrial Economics,* vol. 5 (November 1956), pp. 63-67.

carry for only one customer with whom the carrier must have a long-term contract (over a year). Each license specified the number of authorized vehicles. No regulation of rates was imposed.

The "C" license was to be issued without restriction; it could be refused only if the applicant had previously had a "C" license suspended or revoked. In issuing "A" and "B" licenses the licensing authorities were required to consider "the interests of the public generally, including those of persons requiring, as well as those of persons providing facilities for transport." [11] They were required to take into account objections that the license would lead to overprovision of transport. Holders of all licenses must meet conditions on safety, construction, and vehicle use, as well as pay appropriate wages and provide proper working conditions.

The licensing system did not change significantly between 1933 and the passage of the 1968 act. "A" licenses authorized the use of vehicles for hire or reward. The vehicles with "A" licenses could be used anywhere and for any product, and because they were severely restricted in number, they were quite valuable. The Committee on Carriers' Licensing (the "Geddes Committee"; see further below) found that "A" licenses had sold for up to £300 a licensed ton (or about $6,500 at current prices) for a vehicle weighing five tons unladen.[12] But the applicant for an "A" license had to make a declaration of the main work he intended to do and this work was then referred to as carrying for his "normal user." [13] The declaration usually referred only to traffic outward from his home base. As long as he continued to carry for his "normal user" the license-holder was free to carry other goods and work for other people, especially on an incidental basis. However, if the "normal user" was no longer serviced or if a substantial proportion of the work was not done for the normal user then the license-holder might lose his license.

The licensing authorities were free to limit the "B" license vehicles in whatever way they saw fit. Usually the holders of "B" licenses were restricted in the kind of goods carried, the person for whom goods could be carried, and the area of operation. In 1936, about 56 percent of these licenses were restricted to a radius of less than thirty miles.[14] However,

---

[11] Great Britain, Ministry of Transport, *Report of the Committee on Carriers' Licensing* (London: Her Majesty's Stationery Office, 1965), p. 19.

[12] Ibid., p. 60.

[13] Ibid., p. 22.

[14] Brian T. Bayliss, *The Small Firm in the Road Haulage Industry* (London: Her Majesty's Stationery Office, 1971), p. 13.

because the "B" licenses could be restricted in these ways, the licensing authorities were freer in issuing them than they were in issuing the "A" licenses. As a consequence, the easiest method of entering the industry was to apply for a "B" license to carry for own-account as well as for hire.

As can be seen from Table GB–3, in the period from 1953 to 1968 there was only a relatively small increase in the number of "A"-licensed vehicles—roughly 16 percent. On the other hand, the number of "B" licensed vehicles increased 63 percent and the number of "A" contract vehicles quadrupled.

Applications for "A" and "B" licenses were published by the licensing authorities in a special journal called *Application and Decision*. The authority had full power to grant the license, to grant it in modified form, or to refuse to grant it. Any person holding an "A" or "B" license could lodge an objection to anyone's application for an "A" or "B" license on any of the following grounds:

(1) that suitable transport facilities, would, if the application were granted, be in excess of requirements;

(2) that any of the conditions of a carrier's license held by the application had not been complied with; or

(3) that the applicant had suffered a conviction for an offense, or prohibition of the use of his vehicles found unserviceable.

Licensing authorities had the power to hold public inquiries. Applications were normally expected to provide evidence from prospective

Table GB–3
NUMBER OF GOODS VEHICLES, BY LICENSE CLASS, 1953 AND 1968

License Class	1953	1968	Percentage Increase
A	89,300	104,000	16.0
A Contract	9,500	38,000	300.0
B	58,800	96,000	63.0
C	798,500	1,236,000	55.0

Source: Brian T. Bayliss, *The Small Firm in the Road Haulage Industry* (London: Her Majesty's Stationery Office, 1971), p. 38.

13

customers who were having difficulty in obtaining suitable transport facilities. The objectors could try to show that they could provide facilities adequate to the customers' needs. The decision of the licensing authority could be appealed to the Transport Tribunal.

Farm vehicles were exempt from the licensing system. A farmer who received a "C" license for his vehicle was free to carry for hire for other farmers.

Reasons for Regulatory Change

In October 1963, Conservative Minister of Transport Ernest Marples appointed a Committee on Carriers' Licensing, chaired by Lord Geddes. The committee's mandate was "in the light of present day conditions, to examine the operation and effect of the system of carriers' licenses first introduced by the Road and Rail Traffic Act of 1933, and as subsequently modified by statute; and to make recommendations." [15]

In April 1964, the Geddes committee presented its report to Labour Minister of Transport Tom Fraser. Its main finding was that

> neither the present system of licensing nor any variant of it based on control of the number of lorries and restriction of what lorries may carry offers a useful way to achieve what we think might be the main aims of government policy in regulating carriage of goods by road. In three respects such licensing acts adversely. It reduces efficiency. It tends to confer positions of privilege. And it tends to add to congestion on the roads.[16]

Consequently, the committee recommended the "abolition of all restrictions on the capacity of the road haulage industry and on the work for which a lorry may be used." [17] The committee recommended the substitution of permits and permit plates to ensure that motor carriers conformed to the necessary safety regulations.

As a result of the Geddes report, in July 1966 the government put out a "White Paper on Transport Policy" in which the Labour government accepted the view that the existing system of carriers' licensing for goods vehicles was wasteful, ineffective, and unduly complicated,

---

[15] Great Britain, Ministry of Transport, *Report of the Committee on Carriers' Licensing*, p. 1.
[16] Ibid., p. 6.
[17] Ibid.

but it did not accept the view that all licensing should be abolished. In the summer of 1967, the Minister of Transport put forth his views of a proper system. His main proposals were embodied in the 1968 Transport Act.

The Effect of the 1968 Act

Table GB–4 presents data on traffic carried by the major modes of transport for the years 1961 through 1972. Most freight is moved by road, and measured by tonnage, about 80 percent went by road in 1961, about 86 percent in 1972. Measured by ton-miles, about 50 percent was carried in trucks in 1961 and about 64 percent in 1972. Deregulation seems to have had little effect on trends in the percentage of traffic moved by road. The table shows that in the two years after implementation of the 1968 act, the percentage carried by road increased somewhat, but it had increased just as rapidly in the period from 1965 to 1967.

On the other hand, the drop in tons carried by railroads in the years 1971–72 was sharper than for any other two-year period from 1961 through 1972. Bulk commodities such as coal, coke, iron, and steel make up the major portion of the products carried by rail, and the decline in tonnage carried by British rail was probably the result of a slowdown in the economy that depressed production of primary goods. Since the tonnage carried by truck grew by a smaller amount than tonnage carried by railroads (see Table GB–5), deregulation cannot explain the fall. In fact, as Table GB–5 shows, the decline in tons carried was fully accounted for by the reduction in tons of coal, coke, iron, and steel produced, whereas tonnage in goods where rail is competitive with trucking actually grew.

As can be seen from Figures GB–1 and GB–2, professional trucking has been expanding more rapidly than own-account haulage. Table GB–6 shows the tons and ton-miles carried by public haulage and own-account by various vehicle sizes. It would appear from the figure that the initial effect of the 1968 act was to stimulate the use of own-account trucking, probably as the result of the new freedom to carry for others on back hauls. However, this initial reaction appears to have been reversed between 1971 and 1972 as professional trucking continued its long-run growth relative to own-account haulage. But

15

Table GB-4
GOODS TRANSPORT IN GREAT BRITAIN, BY MODE, 1961–72

Mode of Transport	1961	1962	1963	1964	1965	1966	1967	1968	1969	1970	1971	1972
						Millions of Tons						
Road	1,240	1,248	1,385	1,535	1,565	1,615	1,625	1,680	1,690	1,686	1,735	1,698
Rail	238	228	235	240	229	214	201	207	207	205	196	175
Coastal shipping	48	48	50	51	53	52	49	48	48	48	46	47
Inland waterways	9	9	9	9	8	8	7	7	7	6	5	5
Pipelines	6	7	15	18	26	31	31	39	43	47	54	51
Total	1,539	1,540	1,694	1,853	1,881	1,920	1,913	1,981	1,995	1,992	2,036	1,976
Percentage carried by road	80.6	81.0	81.8	82.8	83.2	84.1	84.9	84.8	84.7	84.6	85.2	85.9
						Billions of Ton-Miles						
Road	32.3	33.6	35.1	40.2	42.1	44.8	45.6	48.3	49.3	50.0	50.4	51.4
Rail	17.6	16.1	15.4	16.1	15.4	14.8	13.6	14.7	15.3	16.4	14.9	14.2
Coastal shipping	13.5	14.3	14.9	15.1	15.3	15.5	15.2	15.0	14.8	14.2	13.1	13.0
Inland waterways	0.2	0.2	0.1	0.1	0.1	0.1	0.1	0.1	0.1	0.1	0.1	0.1
Pipelines	0.3	0.4	0.5	0.7	0.8	0.9	1.0	1.4	1.6	1.8	2.0	1.9
Total	63.9	64.6	66.0	72.2	73.7	76.1	75.5	79.5	81.1	82.5	80.5	80.6
Percentage carried by road	50.5	52.0	53.2	55.7	57.1	58.9	60.4	60.8	60.8	60.6	62.6	63.8

Source: Great Britain, *Annual Abstract of Statistics, 1972, 1973* (London: Her Majesty's Stationery Office, 1973).

Figure GB–1

ESTIMATED TONS CARRIED BY GOODS VEHICLES
IN GREAT BRITAIN, 1962–72

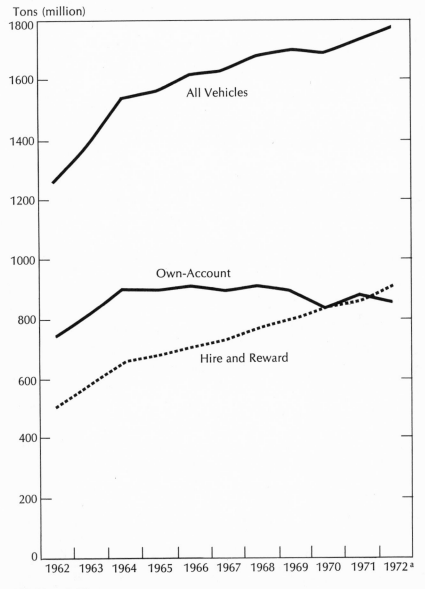

Tons (million)

a First two quarters.
Source: Department of the Environment, Directorate of Statistics, "The Transport of Goods by Road: 1970-1972." Mimeographed.

Table GB-5

BRITISH RAIL PASSENGER AND FREIGHT RECEIPTS AND TRAFFIC, SELECTED YEARS, 1962–72

Item	Unit	1962	1964	1966	1967	1968	1969	1970	1971	1972
Traffic receipts:										
Total[a]	£ Mill.	462.4	468.3	463.8	438.7	456.5	471.6	509.8	532.1	564.2
Passenger:										
Total	£ Thou.	161,138	167,219	179,427	179,701	185,156	205,418	227,766	260,990	274,055
Freight:										
Total	£ Thou.	293,135	291,552	275,237	250,317	262,393	255,547	270,631	258,895	251,986
Coal and coke	£ Thou.	103,189	102,450	99,680	87,818	91,106	92,561	95,990	87,691	77,472
Iron and steel	£ Thou.	34,904	39,453	34,250	30,967	33,342	35,791	38,919	33,141	33,946
Other	£ Thou.	97,598	91,078	82,991	76,039	79,886	67,143	73,314	73,024	71,927
Merchandise by coaching train	£ Thou.	37,479	38,536	36,951	35,062	37,022	38,642	39,518	42,247	42,407
Postal parcels and letter mails	£ Thou.	19,965	20,035	21,365	20,431	21,037	21,410	22,890	22,792	26,239
Miscellaneous receipts	£ Thou.	8,153	9,482	9,105	8,701	8,984	10,607	11,395	12,259	38,151

18

Freight traffic originating:										
Total	Mill. tons	228.4	239.6	213.5	200.7	207.3	207.2	205.4	195.8	175.0
Coal and coke	Mill. tons	145.0	147.4	131.7	122.2	122.7	119.3	112.5	107.5	88.0
Iron and steel	Mill. tons	37.1	45.9	38.8	35.7	38.7	39.4	39.5	33.3	31.2
Other	Mill. tons	46.3	46.3	43.0	42.8	45.9	48.5	53.4	55.0	55.8
Net ton-miles										
Total	Millions	16,104	16,052	14,825	13,609	14,693	15,258	16,394	14,948	14,158
Coal and coke	Millions	7,304	7,470	6,868	5,997	6,277	6,307	6,247	—	—
All other freight traffic	Millions	8,800	8,582	7,957	7,612	8,416	8,951	10,145	—	—

a Grants received by British Rail in respect of certain subsidized passenger services are not included in passenger receipts.

Source: Great Britain, *Annual Abstract of Statistics, 1972, 1973.*

Figure GB–2

ESTIMATED TON-MILES PERFORMED BY GOODS VEHICLES
IN GREAT BRITAIN, 1962–72

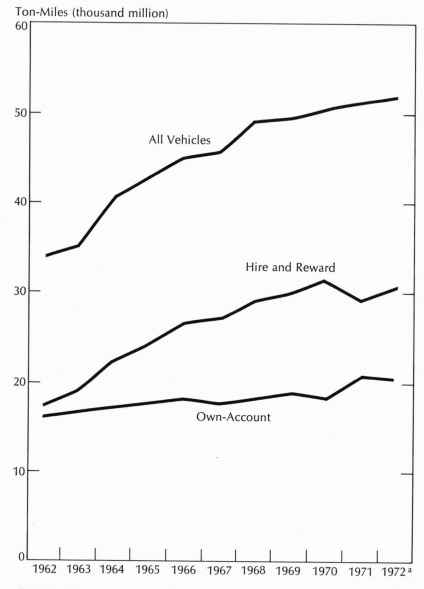

Ton-Miles (thousand million)

a First two quarters.

Source: Department of the Environment, Directorate of Statistics, "The Transport of Goods by Road: 1970-1972." Mimeographed.

20

Table GB–6

TONS AND TON-MILES CARRIED BY PROFESSIONAL AND OWN-ACCOUNT, BY SIZE OF VEHICLE, 1970–72

Unladen Weight of Vehicle (tons)	Tons Carried (millions)			Ton-Miles (billions)		
	1970	1971	1972[a]	1970	1971	1972[a]
Professional						
Less than five[b]	243	252	134	6.6	5.5	3.2
Five to eight	381	345	199	12.6	10.9	5.4
Eight or more	220	267	115	12.4	13.1	6.6
Total	844	864	448	31.6	29.5	15.2
Own-Account						
Less than five[b]	496	430	184	8.8	8.5	3.3
Five to eight	231	230	139	5.9	6.1	3.9
Eight or more	115	211	98	3.7	6.3	3.1
Total	842	871	421	18.3	20.9	10.4
All vehicles						
Less than five[b]	739	682	318	15.4	14.0	6.5
Five to eight	612	575	338	18.4	16.9	9.4
Eight or more	335	478	213	16.1	19.4	9.7
Total	1,686	1,735	869	50.0	50.4	25.6

a First two quarters only.

b Includes an estimate for the work done by those vehicles not covered by operators' licensing and thus not included in the sample.

Source: Department of the Environment, Directorate of Statistics, "The Transport of Goods by Road: 1970–1972."

Table GB–6 indicates that while professional trucking increased its share of the market handled by small trucks (less than 5 tons unladen), own-account gained in its share of the market handled by larger vehicles presumably used on longer hauls. Sources connected with the industry suggest that own-account carriage may drop in the future.[18] Several large own-account firms are converting their trucking departments to separate subsidiaries that will haul for hire and reward.[19] One large

18 Interviews with spokesmen for the Road Haulage Association, the Freight Transport Association, and the Road Transport Industry Training Board, October 1973.

19 *The Economist*, 16 November 1974, survey, p. 29.

shipper who uses some of his own trucks told me of his company's intention to abandon own-account haulage as soon as this is practical.

In spite of the fact that data do not exist on the share of long-distance trucking held by the National Freight Corporation (the nationalized company), it is apparent from Table GB–7 that about one-quarter of the industry's employees works for the National Freight Corporation. The percentage is actually declining as the National Freight Corporation rationalizes its system. The large size of the National Freight Corporation stems from its origin: in 1947 the British Labour government established the Road Haulage Executive to purchase all long-distance trucking firms. This company purchased 81,000 vehicles from trucking firms in a four-year period. As a result of nationalization, own-account trucking grew very rapidly: in four years the number of own-account vehicles ballooned from 384,000 to 727,000.[20]

The Road Haulage Executive was not a success. Often it found that it had purchased a trucking firm's vehicles but not its customers. The former trucking firm would buy new trucks and rent them to its former customers. Since it was illegal to rent trucks and drivers, a separate company would be established that would hire out drivers. Many of the "C"-licensed own-account vehicles were actually professional trucks. The Road Haulage Executive found it difficult to compete with these "own-account" vehicles and with "B"-licensed firms.

In 1953 a Conservative government attempted to return trucking to private hands by setting up a disposal board to sell a good portion of the Road Haulage Executive's vehicles. The government found it was difficult to sell the trucks, and by 1956 only 18,832 of the 25,227 vehicles offered for sale had found purchasers.[21]

The loss in market share by the National Freight Corporation does not appear to be related to the 1968 act. As can be seen from Table GB–8, the National Freight Corporation is not especially profitable, and shippers and competitors told me that it was inefficient and provided poor service. Spokesmen for the National Freight Corporation said that the corporation does not earn much on general haulage: a substantial proportion of its profits comes from contract business and a little from spot haulage.[22] British Road Service, Ltd., the major national-

---

[20] Ibid., pp. 14, 16.

[21] Ibid., p. 17.

[22] Interview with B. Warner, chief of economic and market service, National Freight Corporation, October 1973.

Table GB–7

CONCENTRATION IN ROAD HAULAGE, 1969–73

Unit	1969	1970	1971	1972	1973
	---------------------- As of 31 March ------------------------				
Total firms	13,983	13,717	15,072	14,024	14,000 [a]
Firms with fewer than ten employees	10,702	9,846	11,032	9,904	9,900 [a]
Firms with more than 250 employees	53	78	87	114	135
Percentage of industry employment in firms with over 250 employees		44.0	44.1	42.7	42.3
Total employment in professional road haulage		250,000	249,685	236,420	231,000
Total employed by four largest private firms		9,250	10,487	10,166	10,626
Percentage employed by four largest private firms		3.7	4.2	4.3	4.6
	---------------------- As of 30 December ------------------------				
National Freight Corporation Total number of employees	65,600	63,500	55,400	51,700	
Total employees in general haulage	22,000	21,000	16,900	15,700	
Number of vehicles	29,000	27,800	26,100	24,100	
General haulage vehicles	12,900	12,500	12,200	10,900	
Total vehicle capacity (tons)	252,000	252,000	245,000	226,000	
General haulage vehicle capacity (tons)	150,000	150,000	145,000	129,000	
Average mileage, general haulage vehicles	26,047	25,760	24,500	25,505	

[a] Estimated by Road Transport Industry Training Board.

Source: Data from the Road Transport Industry Training Board, "Report and Statement of Accounts," for various years, and the National Freight Corporation, *Annual Reports.*

23

Table GB-8
SAMPLE OF PROFITS IN ROAD HAULAGE, 1968–72

	1968	1969	1970	1971	1972
Sample of private firms					
Revenue (£)	10,667,305	18,625,053	19,996,508	29,570,502	26,606,374
Profits before taxes (£)	1,072,702	1,942,969	2,066,754	3,915,753	3,295,156
Profits as percentage of revenue	10.1	10.4	10.3	13.2	12.4
Number of firms in sample	8	11	11	12	9
Profits as percentage of total assets	9.5	14.0	14.6	17.8	17.3
Transport Development Group Limited (a large private firm)					
Revenue (£)	27,184,000	31,145,000	36,944,000	40,543,000	43,398,000
Profits before taxes (£)	3,018,000	3,256,000	3,678,000	4,012,000	4,382,000
Profits as percentage of revenue	11.2	10.5	10.0	9.9	10.1
Profits as percentage of total assets	16.0	17.0	18.7	16.0	15.9
National Freight Corporation— general haulage and container companies					
Revenue (£)		75,400,000	86,000,000	82,100,000	85,200,000
Profits (£)		−300,000	1,000,000	2,900,000	1,600,000
Profits as percentage of revenue		−0.4	1.2	3.6	1.9

Profits as percentage of total assets:

British Road Service, Ltd.	1.4	2.3	2.2	3.7	4.3
British Road Service (Contracts) Ltd.	4.2	4.3	5.5	11.7	13.1

Note: These figures should be used with caution. Accounting periods differ within the sample of private firms. In some cases the profits are profits on the whole enterprise; in other cases on haulage only.

Source: Data from the annual reports of following selected companies: the Amey Group Ltd., Victory Transport Ltd., Bullers Transport Co. Ltd., Ralph Hilton Transport Service Ltd., McVeigh Transport Ltd., Humber McVeigh Transport Ltd., United Transport Co. Ltd., Lex Services Group Ltd., United Carriers Ltd., Greenwoods (St. Ives) Ltd., Greenwoods Transport Ltd., Consolidated Land Services (Scunthorpe) Ltd., Hargraves Transport Ltd., Blox Services Ltd., Transport Development Group, the National Freight Corporation, the British Road Service Ltd., and British Road Service (Contracts) Ltd.

ized general carrier, earned a trading profit of only £156,877 on revenue of £36,238,088 (or 4.3 percent on total assets) in 1972, while British Road Service contract carriage earned a profit (after tax) of £1,754,976 on a smaller revenue of £16,842,267.

Figures on the extent of contract carriage in Great Britain generally are nonexistent. It is apparent from discussion with those in the industry that the proportion is not large, although both shippers and carriers expressed an interest in increasing the share of their business done under long-term contract. Even though long-term contracts are rare, most truckers and shippers have regular arrangements that last for considerable periods.

One large shipper reported that as a result of the 1968 act a number of local own-account truckers had expanded their operations to handle other firms' local distribution under contract. He reported no difficulty in finding carriers to handle shipments even to remote parts of northern Scotland. He did report, however, that since passage of the act haulers more often pick up shipments at the factory in a small vehicle, take the shipment to a depot for offloading onto a long-haul truck for the trunk haul to another depot, where the product is offloaded onto a small distribution vehicle. The shipper complained that this resulted in delays in shipment.[23]

Table GB–9 gives the number of entrants into road haulage for every year from 1962 through 1972. Actually these statistics are for the number of new licenses issued in each of the eleven traffic areas, so that many "new" licenses represent expansions of existing firms into new areas. New licenses are also issued whenever there is a transfer of ownership or a change in entity. The number of those granted licenses for professional haulage increased reasonably steadily until 1968. In 1969, small vehicles were exempted from licensing and in 1970 the conversion to the new operators' licenses was begun. The large number of "O" licenses issued in 1971 reflects the fact that both own-account and professional haulers needed "O" licenses, as well as the fact that for the first time farmers were required to get a license. The figures for 1972 are thus the first to show an approximately normal rate of entry. It is true that, according to Bayliss, many farmers failed to apply for licenses in 1971, and the 1972 figure may well be inflated by the late applications of farmers. Bayliss estimates the true new entry for

---

[23] Interview with the shipping manager of a large international corporation, November 1973.

Table GB–9
LICENSES ISSUED TO NEW APPLICANTS, 1962–72

Year	Professional	Own-Account	Operators	Total
1962	11,437	52,538		63,975
1963	12,480	51,161		63,641
1964	14,315	53,631		67,946
1965	11,892	51,404		63,296
1966	15,066	47,799		62,865
1967	14,990	53,755		68,745
1968	15,624	45,902		61,526
1969	14,949	12,303		27,252
1970			5,272	5,272
1971			26,486	26,486
1972			14,818	14,818

Note: The licensing year now ends 30 September. Since the new operator's licensing system began in 1970, figures for that year cover only the period from 31 March to 30 September.
Source: Department of the Environment, "Annual Reports of the Licensing Authorities, 1965–1973," mimeographed (London, 1965–1973).

1971 at about 7,000 with about 3,000 new professional firms entering.[24] It is worth noting that in 1972 the number entering the industry for own-account and professional haulage together was smaller than the number of entrants for professional haulage alone for any year from 1966 to 1969. Fears that the market would be flooded with new firms have not been realized.

In his survey of "new" entrants, Bayliss found that of the 249 genuine new operators about 45 percent were exclusively own-account truckers and 36 percent were exclusively professional truckers (see Table GB–10). Only 19 percent took advantage of the flexibility inherent in the "O" license to carry both on their own account and professionally. These findings were supported by what I found in discussions with the association representing own-account firms: the association claimed that only a small proportion of own-account firms actually engaged actively in both own-account and for-hire trucking,

[24] Ibid., p. 13.

27

Table GB–10

SAMPLE OF NEW OPERATORS, BY EXTENT OF PROFESSIONAL OPERATIONS AND FLEET SIZE, 1971

Percentage of Tonnage Carried for Others	Number of Vehicles in Fleet			Total Vehicles
	One	Two	Three	
0	72	25	15	112
1 to 10	5	1	3	9
11 to 30	12	1	3	16
31 to 50	3	1	—	4
51 to 70	3	1	—	4
71 to 99	10	1	4	15
100	67	13	9	89
Total	172	43	34	249

Source: Bayliss, *Small Firm in the Road Haulage Industry,* p. 14.

although virtually all members had at one time or another, often as a favor, hauled for others.[25]

Exit from the trucking industry can take many forms—from bankruptcy and liquidation to selling the firm. Bayliss reported the reasons given for the surrender of "O" licenses: as can be seen from Table GB–11, about 19 percent of the licenses were surrendered for reasons that may have to do with unprofitability. The most common reason for the surrender of an operator's license was a change in the legal status of the firm, or the takeover of one firm by another firm.

Table GB–12 shows bankruptcies by road haulage, taxi, hire-car firms, and for nonfood retailing, for the years 1967 through 1972. There was a significant jump in the number of bankruptcies in 1972 by both road haulers and taxi and hire-car firms. The years 1971 and 1972 were extremely poor years for road haulage, according to an industry representative.[26] Both of them were recession years—1971 more than 1972. Thus the increase in bankruptcies could be the result either of the new licensing law which facilitated entry or of the recession. Industry spokesmen, including those speaking for the professional

---

[25] Interview with G. Turvey, secretary of the Freight Transport Association, 9 October 1973.

[26] Interview with Russel.

Table GB–11

REASONS FOR SURRENDER OF OPERATORS' LICENSES FOR A SAMPLE OF FORMER HIRE OR REWARD OPERATORS UNDER CARRIERS' LICENSING, 1971

Reason	Number	Percentage
Take-over of business	36	23
Change of legal entity	50	31
License not taken up	2 ⎫	
Transfer of business to another traffic area	5 ⎬	6
Ill-health, retirement, death	3 ⎭	
Bankrupt	2 ⎫	
Liquidation	6 ⎬	19
Out of Business	22 ⎭	
License current	34	21
Total	160	100

Source: Bayliss, *Small Firm in the Road Haulage Industry*, p. 17.

Table GB–12

COMPARISON OF BANKRUPTCIES BY ROAD HAULERS AND OTHERS, 1967–72

	Number of Cases		
Year	Road haulers	Taxi and hire-car firms	Nonfood retailing
1967	117	49	
1968	123	51	
1969	112	63	
1970	114	63	548
1971	128	62	455
1972	146	74	436

Source: Data from a letter to the author from a representative in the Bankruptcy Department, United Kingdom Department of Trade and Industry.

truckers, attributed the poor year not to the licensing law but to the recession in business activity. It is significant that the number of bankruptcies in the taxi and hire-car business in these two years was 32 percent higher than the previous four years while the number of bankruptcies in road haulage was up only 21 percent. During the period, there was no change in the laws governing taxi and hire-car firms.

Concentration is not high in road haulage although it does appear to have increased recently. Table GB–7 presents data on concentration for the years from 1970 to 1973 and shows that the percentage of employees in the industry employed by the four largest firms increased steadily to nearly 5 percent in 1973. If the employees of the National Freight Corporation are excluded, the four largest private firms have about 5.9 percent of the total private employment in professional trucking. The number of firms having more than 250 employees has grown rapidly. By the beginning of October 1973 it had reached 149 firms, many of them likely to be own-account operators that under the new law converted to professional haulage.[27] It can be seen that the number of small firms with less than ten employees jumped significantly in 1971, the first year under the "O" licensing system. The number then retreated to a level lower than the level before the implementation of the new system. In interpreting Table GB–7, it should be kept in mind that the data for the National Freight Corporation are for the end of the calendar year. Table GB–13 presents data on the concentration of the industry according to number of vehicles for the year 1969. Unfortunately there do not appear to be more recent data for comparison with these figures.

Table GB–14 gives data on the size distribution of professional road haulage firms. The numbers of firms in the two largest size classes have grown steadily in recent years, whereas smaller size classes have either shrunk or presented a mixed picture. By the survivor principle— that is, the principle that the number of firms of uneconomic size will dwindle and the number of firms of economic size will grow—it might be concluded that only firms in the two largest size classes are economically efficient.

The growth in the number and size of large firms began long before 1968. Spokesmen for the two trade associations—one for the

---

[27] Interview with D. C. Barnett, divisional manager, Planning and Intelligence Division, Road Transport Industry Training Board, October 1973.

Table GB–13
ROAD HAULAGE FLEETS BY SIZE, 1969

Size of Fleet (number of vehicles)	Professional		Own-Account	
	Percentage of operators	Percentage of vehicles	Percentage of operators	Percentage of vehicles
One	48	10	57	13
Two to five	34	21	33	21
Six to twenty	14	30	8	19
Twenty-one to fifty		17		10
Fifty-one to 100	4	7	2	8
Over 100		15		29
Total	100	100	100	100

Source: Department of the Environment, Minister for Transport Industries, *Lorries and the World We Live In* (London: Her Majesty's Stationery Office, 1973), p. 47.

haulers and one for the major shippers and own-account operators—did not think that the 1968 act had stimulated mergers or promoted the growth of large trucking firms.[28] They looked at the recent growth as a continuation of a long-term trend. On the other hand, one large shipper did attribute the growth of the large firms to the new flexibility possible under the "O" system. It is impossible to be sure of the impact of the 1968 act on concentration and the distribution of firms by size. Since there seems to be a divergence of opinion and since the figures do not indicate that the rate of growth in the number of large firms or in the four largest firms has increased, it is probably best to conclude that any effect of the 1968 act has been marginal.

As the figures indicate, in 1973 there were about 13,000 small- and medium-sized firms (fifty or fewer employees). Most of them were firms that specialize in handling a particular kind of traffic and in serving a particular geographic region.

A survey concluded by Brian Bayliss found that 48 percent of those firms with only one vehicle operated within a 30-mile radius and only 8 percent operated beyond a 125-mile radius.[29] On the other hand only

[28] Interviews with Turvey and Russel.

[29] *The Road Haulage Industry since 1968* (London: Her Majesty's Stationery Office, 1973), p. 22.

Table GB-14

SIZE DISTRIBUTION OF ROAD HAULAGE FIRMS, 1969–73

Size of Firms (number of employees)	Number of Firms					Number of Employees			
	1969	1970	1971	1972[a]	1973[a]	1970	1971	1972	1973
5 or fewer	9,160	7,688	8,942	7,534	n.a.	14,000	13,469	16,335	n.a.
5 to 10	1,542	2,158	2,090	2,370	n.a.	16,000	15,731	13,214	n.a.
11 to 15	913	1,182	1,158	1,025	949	14,300	14,147	10,332	9,289
16 to 50	1,853	2,032	2,133	2,541	2,202	48,700	48,416	35,210	43,222
51 to 250	462	579	662	683	819	47,000	47,751	51,656	50,031
Over 250	53	78	87	114	135	110,000	110,171	100,989	97,930
Total	13,983	13,717	15,072	14,024	14,000	250,000	249,685	236,420	231,000

[a] As of 31 March.

Source: Data from the Road Transport Industry Training Board, "Report and Statement of Accounts" for various years.

16 percent of the large firms with over fifty vehicles confined themselves to a 30-mile radius while 42 percent operated beyond 125 miles. Table GB–15 indicates the degree of specialization by commodity. As can be seen, small firms tend to be highly specialized, with only a small percentage operating generally. Larger firms, especially those with eleven to twenty vehicles or twenty-one to fifty vehicles, are much more likely to be general operators. Over half of the one-vehicle firms are in building and construction and the tipping business (sand and gravel).

Trucking firms are usually listed in a directory organized geographically and showing the points the firm will serve, the kinds of vehicles available, the frequency of service, and any limitations on the kinds of cargo handled. In each area there are one or more clearing houses (often trucking firms) to which a hauler looking for a return load can go. Neither shippers nor truckers like to deal with the clearing houses. Most shippers prefer to know the trucking firm they are dealing with. Use of a clearing house means that the shipper's goods will go by whatever carrier needs a return load in his direction. On the other hand, clearing houses are usually cheaper than known trucking firms. Truckers do not like to deal with clearing houses because the rates they receive are low and the clearing houses often pay the trucker only after a considerable delay. Yet the clearing houses stay in business because they provide low rates for those who do not care about speed or who do not care who moves their goods, and because they make it possible for truckers far from home to get return loads.

Many of the smallest firms are exclusively in the sand and gravel business and usually operate only locally. This is one of the most competitive sectors of the industry, since entry is easy and capital requirements low. Other small firms work exclusively for a single shipper and are in fact employees of a larger firm, although in law they are independent entrepreneurs.

The fears that, without regulation, excessive competition would develop in trucking have not been realized. There are a number of reasons for this. Shippers normally prefer to know their hauler and to use experienced haulers, so that entry for a newcomer is not easy and rate cutting is unlikely to bring much business unless the firm can demonstrate competence and reliability. Truckers looking for backhauls do not in fact reduce rates below profitable levels because shippers want to deal with operators they know.

Table GB–15

PROFESSIONAL TRUCKERS, BY MAIN TYPE OF WORK AND FLEET SIZE, 1971

Percentage Distribution

Size of Firm (number of vehicles)	Smalls and parcels	Building and construction	Bulk liquids	Food stuffs	Agricultural	Tipping	Manufacturing	Other	General
1	2	24	—	2	10	29	5	13	15
2	—	19	5	6	15	29	3	13	10
3 to 5	1	17	2	4	13	26	5	13	19
6 to 10	—	14	4	3	13	15	6	12	33
11 to 20	7	4	4	9	9	18	4	5	40
21 to 50	3	10	3	4	—	13	7	10	50
Over 50	11	5	16	16	—	5	16	5	26

Source: Bayliss, *Small Firm in the Road Haulage Industry*, p. 22.

Even though there are about 14,000 professional trucking firms in Great Britain, most of them do not compete with each other although there is no legal barrier to doing so. Potential competition is obviously great. It would appear that about 12.5 percent or roughly 1,800 firms operate over distances greater than 125 miles.[30] Long-haul trucking firms are divided into those in the parcels business, those in the tanker business (further subdivided into petroleum products, chemicals, food and milk, beer, and so on), livestock carriers, and general haulage. Finally, most firms restrict themselves to certain routes or areas. As a consequence, a shipper with special requirements may find only one or two firms ready to meet his needs on short notice.

Historical data on industry revenues, profits, and the return on investment do not exist. There are income tax figures on taxable profits for road haulage but the latest available data are for 1968 and therefore of no help in judging the effect of the 1968 act. However, I have collected figures for a sample of medium- to large-sized corporations engaged in road haulage. These numbers must be considered only indicative of the state of the industry. It should be recognized that this group does not reflect a truly random sample, though it is not biased as far as I know. Most of the names of the companies concerned were provided by the Road Haulage Association.

The data for each firm were taken from the firm's annual reports. In most cases the firms reported their figures on a calendar-year basis. For those firms whose fiscal year ended before April, the figures were attributed to the previous year. Wherever possible, trading profits on transport were used. In two cases, total before-tax profits for an operating subsidiary involved in haulage were used. In all cases it was possible to get road haulage revenue (turnover).

The results of this investigation are shown in Table GB–8 above. Surprisingly enough, considering the difficulties with the data and considering that profits vary greatly, total profits each year for the sample were a reasonable and consistent proportion of total turnover. It is especially interesting to note that, for this sample, the change in licensing law does not seem to have had any noticeable effect on profit rates, though it may be observed that in fact profit rates were higher for 1971 and 1972 than for earlier years. In terms of a return on capital, profits appear to have grown over the period, although the sample is small and

---

[30] Computed on the basis of statistics in ibid., pp. 19 and 22.

Table GB–16

PROFITS AS PERCENTAGE OF REVENUE
IN 1965 AND 1971, BY SIZE OF FIRM

Size of Firm (number of vehicles)	Profits as Percentage of Revenue		Percentage Change
	1965	1971	
One[a]	54	46	—15
Two[b]	—	27	—
Three to five	13	13	0
Six to ten	24	24	0
Eleven to twenty	24	15	—37
Twenty-one to fifty	12	13	+8
Over fifty	6	14	+133
All firms larger than two vehicles	15	15	0

[a] Profits for one vehicle include all wages.
[b] Profits for two vehicles include managerial wages and are not comparable between 1965 and 1971.
Source: Bayliss, *Small Firm in the Road Haulage Industry,* pp. 25, 26.

not too much should be made of the data. One firm, the Transport Development Group Ltd., was so much larger than any other that its data were kept separate from the sample. However, its rate of profit was about the same as the rate of profit for the smaller firms. It is especially interesting to compare these figures with the data for the National Freight Corporation, which showed a loss the first year and a noticeably low rate of profit for ensuing years.

Bayliss's study of the road haulage industry confirms the view that deregulation did not depress profits. He found that costs as a percentage of revenue for all firms with more than two vehicles remained unchanged at 85 percent.[31] Thus for his much larger sample (which included medium-sized as well as large firms), profits did not change. Table GB–16 gives his findings.

Haulage rates are freely negotiated in the United Kingdom and always have been. Published rates are common in the parcels business

---

[31] Ibid., pp. 25-26.

Figure GB–3

RATE PER TON TO SHIP GOODS 100 MILES
(April 1973 £)

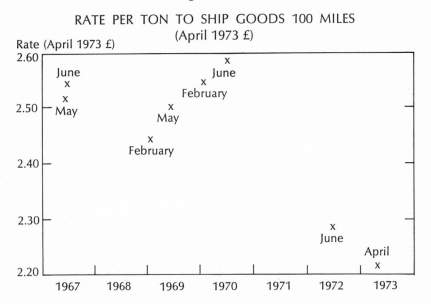

Note: Each X represents a new rate. Between the Xs the nominal rate remained constant and the real rate declined.

Source: Data from the files of a large British company.

but often serve only as a starting point for any negotiations by a large shipper. Surprisingly, these rates have tended to be stable for reasonably long periods of time. For example, one shipper reported no price change at all for either the year 1969 or the year 1971.[32] It may be noted that the Road Haulage Association does publish recommended rates which are often used as a starting point in negotiations. Reputedly, parcels companies collude on rates.

Figure GB–3 shows rates per ton in constant pounds for shipment 100 miles from a plant of a large British company. Between the points the nominal rate after taking account of inflation would have declined. The rates for 1972 and 1973 are considerably lower than the rates for earlier years.

Table GB–17 presents an index of the rates charged a large company based in Britain for different products and for different distances. After inflation is taken into account, the index shows that rates declined in 1972 and 1973 following a steady increase for previous years.

[32] Confidential data provided by one large shipping firm.

Table GB–17

INDICES OF FREIGHT RATES PAID BY ONE SHIPPER, 1967–73
(in constant pounds, 1967 = 100)

Year	Bulk Liquid 18½ to 19½ tons (per ton-mile)	Finished Product	
		80 miles	300 miles
1967	100	100	100
1968	105.6	107.0	102.8
1969	107.5	108.9	103.2
1970	107.5	117.1	102.1
1971	108.8	119.6	103.9
1972	106.2	111.4	97.2
1973	102.5	102.6	93.6

Source: Data from the files of a large U.S. company operating in Great Britain.

There are two probable explanations for the fall in real rates. In November 1972 the British government instituted a six-month price freeze. This action, of course, might have held rates down, although its effect would only have been significant if a large increase would have taken place after November. The other explanation is that increased competition, coupled with the new freedom involved in "O"-licensing, in fact reduced costs and rates. Probably Phase II of the British incomes policy (which went into effect in May 1973) had an effect on rates in 1973. Phase II permitted an average rate increase of 5 percent, although truckers were allowed to increase some rates by more than 5 percent if they held other rate increases to less than 5 percent.

In the small-consignment market several companies offer premium service at premium prices, but the largest firms do not. One firm offers delivery within most of Great Britain before noon the next day at very high rates (service A). Next-day delivery before 5:30 P.M. (service B) is cheaper, and 48-hour delivery (service C) is cheaper still. The charge for the 48-hour service (which is not much if any faster than the service offered by ordinary parcel companies) is significantly higher than the charge for service provided by other companies and as a consequence the service is not much used. Table GB–18 shows some sample rates for 1973; one other major company would have carried an eleven-pound consignment 100 to 200 miles at about one-quarter of the service C rate.

Table GB–18
PREMIUM SERVICE RATES
(contract, in pounds)

	Eleven lbs. for—		Forty-four lbs. for—	
	0 to 100 miles	100 to 200 miles	0 to 100 miles	over 450 miles
Service A	3.40	3.70	5.00	6.55
Service B	2.10	2.50	3.90	5.60
Service C	1.95	2.20	3.40	5.10

Source: Confidential report of a consulting firm prepared for a parcel goods carrier, 1974.

Figures given by the Freight Transport Association regarding the cost of operating various kinds and sizes of trucks show a decline in real costs since 1970, the first year the data were collected. The decline in real rates for shipping ten tons of finished product for both the 80-mile distance and the 300-mile distance has been larger than the decline in costs for operating a truck that would carry that load. Because these cost figures do not include overhead or loading costs, not much significance can be attributed to this divergence in costs and rates, and the divergence is not large in any case.

Conclusion

The effect of the 1968 Transport Act on the British trucking industry has not been great. Profits apparently have remained stable, the industry has not been flooded with new entrants, prices have tended to decline, and service quality has been little affected. Long-term trends in concentration and in freight movements have continued. Discussions with industry representatives suggest no great unhappiness with the act, although there was the desire that it be made easier to object to an application for an "O" license. Shippers seem generally happy with the results of deregulation.

2
Regulation in West Germany

In 1931 Germany instituted regulation of the road haulage industry by establishing comprehensive rate control that tied truck rates to rail rates. Later, in 1935, capacity control was imposed.

The main objective of German regulation was the protection of rail traffic. As in most other countries, the combination of the Depression and the rapid growth of the road haulage industry had reduced railroad earnings. The road haulage industry took the most profitable traffic, leaving the railroads with uneconomic traffic, much of which the government required the railroads to carry at a loss. The reduction in earnings of the German state railroad was most disturbing because, for a hundred years, the profits of this railroad had financed the government. Because reduced earnings—and indeed losses—produced financial problems for the government, steps were taken to protect the railroads. Yet, despite regulation, the problems have become more acute in recent years. In 1971 the deficit of the federal railroad reached about 2.7 billion DM (about $1 billion).[1]

The secondary objective of bringing road haulage under regulation was to reduce competition in order to stabilize the road haulage industry. Before regulation, entry into the road haulage industry had been so easy that with the advent of massive unemployment, those who were desperate to earn a living anywhere flocked to the trucking industry. The result was a highly competitive market, a rapid turnover of firms, and low profits (or none at all) for many operators.

[1] *Verkehrs-Wirtschaftliche Zahlen 1972* (Frankfurt: Bundesverband des Deutschen Güterfernverkehrs, 1973).

Postwar regulation of the road haulage industry is based on the Road Haulage Act of 17 October 1952, which (with minor modifications) still controls the trucking industry in West Germany. According to West German law, the trucking industry is divided into long-distance transport—for distances over 50 kilometers—and short-distance transport. Because the purpose of regulation was to protect the railroads, short-distance transport is much less controlled than long-distance transport.

The Road Haulage Act of 1952 established both capacity control and rate control for long-distance professional transport. Capacity control limits the number of vehicles that a road haulage firm is permitted to operate, and vehicles used in West Germany are in turn restricted to a maximum gross weight of thirty-eight metric tons. Four kinds of vehicle licenses are issued: long-distance, regional, furniture removals, and international. (See Table WG–1 for the number of such licenses

Table WG–1
NUMBER OF VEHICLE LICENSES HELD BY LONG-DISTANCE ROAD HAULAGE FIRMS, VARIOUS DATES, 1960–70

Item	August 1960	April 1964	July 1966	July 1970
Number of vehicle licenses per firm				
One	5,838	4,972	4,639	3,774
Two	5,310	5,036	5,108	4,620
Three	3,342	3,321	3,741	3,651
Four to six	5,377	5,737	6,629	6,658
Seven to ten	2,830	3,405	4,176	4,489
Eleven and over	3,017	3,461	4,942	6,295
Total licenses	25,714	25,932	29,235	29,487
Type of licenses				
All West Germany	15,875	16,030	17,298	17,432
International	—	—	995	994
Regional	6,010	6,040	6,524	6,601
Furniture removals	3,829	3,862	4,418	4,460

Source: *Verkehrs-Wirtschaftliche Zahlen 1972* (Frankfurt: Bundesverband des Deutschen Güterfernverkehrs, 1973).

permitted and the year the number was changed.) Long-distance licenses permit the operator to use the vehicle anywhere in the country, although periodic returns must be made to the *Land* (that is, the Federal State) of issue. Since 1 January 1973, each of the 17,432 long-distance licenses has been transferable from one vehicle to another. It is simply required that each vehicle operating for hire or reward on the road carry one of these licenses at all times.

The 6,601 regional licenses permit vehicles to travel within a 150-kilometer radius of their base. The 994 international licenses entitle the holder to cross frontiers and, for each trip out of the country, one domestic trip is permitted. The 4,460 furniture-removal licenses, as the name suggests, authorize the holder to carry furniture and household goods anywhere within West Germany in specially built trucks and trailers.

Theoretically the requirements for obtaining a license are that the applicant be personally reliable, have a specialist's knowledge of the industry, and be capable of the undertaking, and that the license be compatible with the public interest in the "maintenance of a regulated long distance transport." But in fact, since the number of licenses is fixed by ministerial decree, there are no licenses available for any applicant. All the states keep a list of applicants, and when the federal government decides to increase the number of licenses the licenses are allocated essentially on a first-come, first-served basis. The lists are quite long.

Once a license has been acquired, a firm or individual does not voluntarily relinquish it. Given the fact that licenses are restricted in number and rates are controlled, a license has a considerable value. Officially, to be sure, the licenses cannot be sold, but a firm with a license can be purchased, and there are brokers who advertise to buy and sell such licenses. No statistics exist on the value of licenses, but it is widely known that the value has fluctuated considerably over time. In the fall of 1973, I was told by someone actively engaged in purchasing licenses that the pure value of a long-distance license was 110,000 DM (over $40,000) for one issued in North Rhine-Westphalia and about 60,000 DM (about $25,000) for one issued in West Berlin.[2] The value of a West Berlin license is considerably depressed because of a requirement that the vehicle being licensed must operate out of West Berlin,

---

[2] Private conversation with a major truck operator who was actively increasing the size of his operation.

which has considerably more goods coming in than going out. A regional license in 1973 was worth about 40,000 to 60,000 DM depending on the region.

Before 1961 road haulage freight rates were tied to railroad freight rates, but since 1961 road haulage rates have been allowed to move separately. In addition, beginning in 1964, upper and lower rates, or (as they are often called) margin rates, were introduced.[3] These margin rates were introduced because of efforts by the European Economic Commission to standardize rate control throughout the Common Market. By 1970 the margin had been increased to plus or minus 6 percent and covered all commodity classes.[4] In April 1972 the margin was increased to 8.5 percent either way and to minus 5 percent and plus 10 percent for the less-than-lorry loads.[5] Currently the rates for shipments of less than 5 tons permit rates to go up 11.5 percent or down 20 percent. These price regulations are policed carefully by the Bundesanstalt für den Güterfernverkehr (BAG), the federal regulatory agency (literally, the Federal Agency for Long-Distance Transport). Copies of all invoices and documents are sent to the BAG, which also has authority to audit books and to make spot checks of vehicles on the highways.

In the year from April 1972 through March 1973, some 65 percent of all shipments were made at rates near or at the bottom of the margins, while only 0.3 percent were made at rates above the regular tariff (see Table WG–2). Actual rates for parcels, however, tended to be in the upper part of the margin except for rates charged regular large-volume customers.

Besides the tariffs in the seven major classifications, road haulage firms are permitted to negotiate exceptional tariffs for movements to ports. As Table WG–2 shows, in 1971 26 percent of the tons shipped and 22 percent of the ton-kilometers accounted for moved on exceptional tariffs. Rates on these exceptional tariffs were generally lower than the major tariff classifications permit.

Proposals for rate changes are initiated by the rate commission, which represents road haulage firms, and users are asked to comment.

---

[3] Bundesverband des Deutschen Güterfernverkehrs, "50 Jahre Güterfernverkehr mit Lastkraftwagen, 25 Jahre Organisation des Güterverkehrs" [Fifty years of long-distance freight transport by truck, twenty-five years of freight transport regulation] (Frankfurt am Main, September 1972), p. 30.

[4] Ibid.

[5] Ibid.

Table WG–2
USE OF MARGINS FOR INDIVIDUAL SHIPMENTS

Period	No deviation	−5%	−6%	−7 to 8.5%	+5%	+6%	+7 to 8.5%
				Percentage Deviation from Tariff			
----- Regular tariff—10 tons -----							
4/72–3/73	26.3	5.8	5.6	62.0	0.2	0.1	0.1
4/71–3/72	32.2	9.7	57.7	—	0.1	0.1	—
5/70–3/71	37.2	12.2	50.4	—	0.1	0.1	—
----- Regular tariff—20 tons -----							
4/72–3/73	20.6	6.1	4.7	68.2	0.1	0.2	0.1
4/71–3/72	31.8	13.3	54.5	—	0.2	0.2	—
5/70–5/71	41.8	15.2	42.7	—	0.2	0.1	—
----- Exceptional tariffs -----							
4/72–3/73	14.3	6.2	12.1	67.2	0.1	—	—
4/71–3/72	18.4	11.8	69.7	—	0.1	0.1	—
5/70–3/71	18.6	21.3	60.0	—	—	0.1	—

Note: Before April 1972 the greatest deviation permitted was 6 percent.
Source: Bundesverand der Deutschen Industrie, mimeographed report (Bonn, 1973).

Approval of the proposed changes is given by the Ministry of Transport after consultation with the Ministry of Economics. In practice, whenever the users have agreed with the proposal of the rate commission, the Ministry of Economics has approved the rate changes.[6] If the users disagree, a compromise is possible.

Long-distance transport on own-account requires a permit for vehicles larger than 4 tons' carrying-capacity and for tractors with over 55 horsepower. Applications for permits must be made to the BAG in Cologne. The application is published and professional road haulage carriers and the railroads are permitted to make offers to carry the goods the firm wants moved. If the federal railroad offers to carry the goods within the same time, giving the same service at the same cost as the applicant expects to achieve, then the law permits the application to be denied and the firm to be directed to use the railroads. However, these

[6] Interview with Detlef Winter, district director in the Ministry of Transport, November 1973.

conditions are almost never met and this provision in the statutes is almost a dead letter.[7]

According to the BAG's interpretation of the law, each firm (each legal person, that is) is allowed to carry its own goods but a wholly-owned subsidiary cannot carry for its parent. This interpretation is being challenged in two lawsuits.[8]

Before 1972 the federal government levied a discriminatory tax on own-account operations. For trucks and trailers with a capacity of less than 4 metric tons the tax was 3 pfennig (pf) per ton-km; for a capacity of 4 to 6 tons, the tax was 4 pf/ton-km; for larger-capacity vehicles the tax was 5 pf/ton-km. This meant that a large vehicle carrying around 400,000 ton-kms per year would pay extra taxes of about 20,000 DM (approximately $8,000). The tax was removed when a West German court ruled that it violated the Common Market treaty. The ruling has stimulated the use of own-account haulage considerably (see Table WG–3). For example, the transport of petroleum products and building materials on own-account, which was affected particularly adversely by the tax, almost doubled in the year after the removal of the tax, as can be seen from Table WG–9 below.

Short-distance truck transport is less rigidly regulated than long-distance truck transport. Professional short-distance road haulage requires a license but there is no quota limiting issue of the licenses. To get a license for short-distance transport, the applicant must be reliable, pass a specialist's examination, and have the capacity to do the work. Licenses are relatively easy to get, and most large firms operating in long-distance transport also have licenses for short-distance haulage. If a hauler licensed for short-distance professional operation is within 50 kilometers of the border, he may operate internationally. Own-account operations of less than 50 kilometers are completely unrestricted, provided the firm is carrying its own goods in its own vehicles driven by its own drivers.

Legal tariffs are established by a local rate commission which consists of local haulers and users. If they cannot agree, a neutral member is appointed by the Ministry of Transport. Licensed short-distance haulers are allowed to cut the basic short-distance rate by as much as 40 percent. In addition, since there is no group to enforce

---

[7] Interview with K. Schöne of the Bundesverband Werkverkehr und Verlader, Bonn, November 1973.
[8] Ibid.

Table WG-3
WEST GERMAN FREIGHT TRAFFIC, BY MODE, 1950–72

	1950	1960	1965	1966	1967	1968	1969	1970	1971	1972
	Millions of Metric Tons									
Railroads	208.8	315.7	311.4	306.9	301.4	331.1	366.8	378.0	348.9	353.6
Road haulage, long distance	32.9	99.2	133.3	137.4	136.9	152.4	157.8	164.9	174.2	192.9
Professional	19.6	71.3	88.4	88.5	84.8	93.1	100.5	104.8	107.6	112.3
Own-account	13.3	23.5	34.1	36.8	38.8	44.6	40.9	41.1	44.8	53.0
Road haulage, short distance	375.0	1,065.0	1,510.0	1,610.0	1,660.0	1,780.0	1,870.0	1,970.0	2,060.0	2,140.0
Professional	155.0	480.0	660.0	680.0	695.0	715.0	740.0	770.0	795.0	820.0
Own-account	220.0	585.0	850.0	930.0	965.0	1,065.0	1,130.0	1,200.0	1,265.0	1,320.0
Inland water carriers	71.9	172.0	195.7	207.9	214.4	233.3	233.8	240.0	230.0	228.5
Total, all modes	714.3	1,742.5	2,296.1	2,417.7	2,473.0	2,687.1	2,826.2	2,974.4	3,031.7	3,220.0
	Billions of Metric Ton-Kilometers									
Railroads	39.4	53.1	58.2	56.9	54.8	59.0	67.6	71.5	65.6	65.2
Road haulage, long distance	7.1	23.7	32.6	33.5	33.9	37.7	39.9	41.9	44.5	49.2
Professional	4.9	18.5	23.3	23.2	22.7	25.3	27.5	28.7	29.4	30.9
Own-account	2.2	3.9	5.8	6.3	6.8	7.8	7.3	7.4	8.2	9.5
Inland water carriers	16.7	40.4	43.6	45.1	45.8	47.9	47.7	48.8	45.6	44.0
Total, all modes	205.5	670.8	794.0	817.9	825.6	1,022.3	1,044.9	1,125.0	1,108.1	1,079.2

Source: West Germany, Ministry of Transport, *Verkehr in Zahlen 1973* (Bonn, 1973).

short-distance tariffs, in effect they can be cut as much as a hauler is willing to cut them.

The Effects of Regulation

It has already been pointed out that one effect of regulation has been to put a high value on long-distance licenses—though the value, as might be expected, has fluctuated over time. According to Brian Bayliss the value of a long-distance license was only 5,000 DM to 10,000 DM in 1965–66.[9] Apparently the value rose until it reached about 100,000 DM in 1969, then fell, and has now climbed to about 110,000 DM in the best markets.[10] These fluctuations reflect changes in capacity regulation. In July 1965 the maximum legal size for a truck was increased by 18.8 percent, from a gross weight of 32 metric tons to a gross weight of 38 metric tons. Apparently this increase almost entirely eliminated the monopoly gains from possession of a vehicle license. However, as demand grew and industry capacity remained fixed at the new level, the value of a license climbed. By the fall of 1973 the value of a license in some of the most important West German states was as high as 110,000 DM.

Naturally, those who buy licenses will only pay these large sums if they expect to be able to earn a sufficient amount from using the license to repay their investment. One buyer reported that he expected to have his investment back in five years. On this basis it is possible to estimate that trucking rates are about 11 percent higher in West Germany than they would be under competitive market conditions.[11] We will see from the chapter comparing the various European countries that West German rates are inflated above rates in countries having fewer restrictions by a margin considerably greater than 11 percent. Since regulation by fostering nonprice competition may increase costs, it is possible that monopoly profits amount to only 11 percent of revenue while trucking rates are 40 to 50 percent higher than competitive rates.

[9] Brian T. Bayliss, "Licensing and Entry to the Market," *Transportation Planning and Technology*, vol. 2 (1973), p. 43.

[10] See footnote 2.

[11] In the calculation, each license was valued at its market price. For a five-year payback, the necessary pretax annual return on the licenses is 20 percent of total value, which is equal to 11 percent of industry revenue.

48

Table WG–4

SURVEY OF WHY GERMAN FIRMS USE
OWN-ACCOUNT VEHICLES

Reason Given	Percentage of Firms Giving Reason
(1) Permanent capability to ship quickly	57
(2) Drivers performed associated services such as installation, repair, and loading	44
(3) Freight rates	40
(4) Better prevention of damages	36
(5) Less packaging cost	32
(6) Advertising on trucks	30
(7) Poor service in remote areas	15
(8) Specialized trucks that are not offered by professional truckers	13

Source: Furnished by Schöne of the Bundesverband Werkverkehr und Verlader, Bonn.

The overall quality of service is high in West Germany. Average turn-around time for a vehicle used in long-distance transportation is 1.8 days.[12] Almost half of the transportation is done at night so that delivery can be made the next day. One firm handling parcels claims to offer twenty-four to forty-eight hour service throughout West Germany.[13] (This firm also charges premium rates for guaranteed quick service.) Nevertheless, there is evidence that service to out-of-the-way areas is not particularly good. In one survey (see Table WG–4) it was found that 15 percent of firms doing their own hauling say they do so because of a need to ship to areas which professional truckers will not serve. If anything, the greater profitability of serving some areas seems to make truckers unwilling to serve less profitable points. Several experts connected with the government and the road haulage industry acknowledged that there was a problem in getting common carriers to

---

12 Interview with a representative of the Bundesverband des Deutschen Güterfernverkehrs, Frankfurt, November 1973.
13 Interview with Helmut Frech of Spedition Frech, 5 December 1973.

take shipments to places near the East German border where backhauls were unlikely to be found.[14]

Surprisingly, profit rates do not appear to be particularly high in West Germany. One executive of a major trucking firm reported that typical profits were on the order of 3 percent to 7 percent of revenue. Government statistics collected in a sample study indicate profits running from 7.7 to 12.0 percent of revenue for long-distance and short-distance firms (see Table WG–5).

Interestingly, profit rates (before taxes) seem to be inversely correlated with size. Unfortunately no data exist that would relate profits to investment, but since the largest firms are probably the most capital intensive they would be expected to have higher profits as a percent of revenue. Even excluding the smallest classes (in which profits are in part paid in salaries of the owner-operators), we find that the inverse correlation for the three largest classes is quite marked (Table WG–5). This would indicate some diseconomies of scale, although other evidence does not support this supposition.[15]

It is significant that profit rates are consistently higher for firms operating mainly in the short-distance market than for firms operating mainly in the long-distance market. This is puzzling because limits on entry and rate controls are much more strict in long-distance than they are in short-distance operations. And in fact since a license for long-distance operations sells for a considerable amount but a license for short-distance operations sells for virtually nothing, profit rates would normally be expected to be higher in long-distance than they would be in short-distance. However, it may be that, at the time of the survey in 1971, the value of a license to operate in long-distance transportation may have been substantially depressed. In 1969, a 1 pfennig per ton-km tax was introduced on commercial haulage, and this tax would have affected the profits of long-distance truckers more adversely than it would have affected the profits of short-distance truckers. If long-distance firms had paid the same amount of this haulage tax as short-distance firms, the profit rates for long-distance haulage would have been above those for short-distance haulage, although not by a great deal. In addition, the quota for long-distance licenses was increased a little in 1970. Alto-

---

[14] Interviews with Schöne and Winter.
[15] The survivor technique described in note d of Table C-2, p. 124 indicates the economies of scale.

Table WG–5

SURVEY OF PROFIT RATES FOR PROFESSIONAL ROAD HAULERS, 1971

Revenue Class (millions of DMs)	Number of Firms in Sample	Percentage of Revenue from: Short-distance	Long-distance	Freight forwarding and storage	Profits as Percentage of Revenues
Short-Distance Firms					
1 to 1.99	101	74.5	12.6	2.1	12.0
2 to 4.99	38	68.0	14.7	1.6	9.1
5 to 10	12	57.3	19.7	4.1	8.6
Average		67.9	15.2	2.4	10.2
Long-Distance Firms					
1 to 1.99	180	14.9	76.2	5.0	8.8
2 to 4.99	151	12.4	73.3	9.3	8.4
5 to 10	26	12.2	68.5	13.7	7.7
Average		13.1	73.2	8.9	8.4
Furniture Removals					
1 to 1.99	34	37.0	52.1	8.3	11.9
2 to 5	20	37.4	53.0	4.3	7.6
Average		37.2	52.6	6.1	9.5
Freight Forwarding					
1 to 4.99	31	9.7	16.9	67.5	6.2
5 to 50	25	7.9	14.4	72.4	4.9
Average		8.2	14.8	71.6	5.1
Warehousing					
1 to 5	9	12.3	13.8	68.7	9.2

Note: Averages are weighted by number of firms and size of revenues.
Source: Reihel, *Die Kostenstruktur in der Wirtschaft, III, Verkehrsgewerbe 1971,* pt. 2: *Gerwerblichen Güterkraftverkehr,* in the series on Unternehmen und Arbeits-stätten (Wiesbaden: Statistisches Bundesamt, 1973).

gether 1971 may not have been one of the more profitable years in West German long-distance trucking.

Table WG–6 makes it apparent that there has been a steady trend toward diversification within the transport area but no trend toward

Table WG–6

DIVERSIFICATION OF LONG-DISTANCE ROAD HAULAGE FIRMS, SELECTED YEARS, 1956–70

Type of Firm	1956	1960	1964	1966	1970	Percentage in 1970 of All Firms
	---------- Number of Firms ----------					
Nondiversified	6,654	3,545	2,477	2,261	1,919	20.0
Diversified	5,510	7,744	7,963	8,393	7,695	80.0
Local haulage	2,711	6,297	7,056	7,666	7,039	73.2
Parcels	1,303	1,686	1,718	1,985	1,935	20.1
Removal and storage	787	1,824	1,574	1,245	1,206	12.5
Other transport-related sidelines	1,301	1,367	1,173	1,403	1,323	13.7
Non-transport-related sidelines	709	577	479	561	511	5.3
	---------- Percentage of Firms ----------					
Nondiversified	54.7	31.4	23.7	21.2	20.0	
Diversified, with non-transport-related sidelines	5.8	5.2	4.6	5.3	5.3	

Source: *Die Bundesanstalt für den Güterfernverkehr* (Cologne: Bundesanstalt für den Güterfernverkehr, 1973), p. 138.

purely conglomerate activity. The most significant change has occurred in the number of long-distance firms that have added short-distance haulage. In 1956 only 22 percent of the firms operating long-distance haulage also engaged in short-distance haulage. By 1970 this figure had risen to 73 percent, undoubtedly reflecting the profits available in short-haul traffic together with the ease of entry into that market. The proportion of firms with sidelines in parcels traffic and removal and storage doubled over this period.

While an industry spokesman claimed that the very largest firms, those with over 100 licensed vehicles, were not growing more rapidly than the industry as a whole, published statistics indicate that large firms, those with more than ten licenses, are growing more rapidly than the

Table WG–7

NUMBER OF LONG-DISTANCE ROAD HAULAGE FIRMS, BY NUMBER OF VEHICLE LICENSES, SELECTED DATES

	August 1960	April 1964	July 1966	July 1970
Number of vehicle licenses per firm				
One	5,838	4,972	4,639	3,774
Two	2,655	2,518	2,554	2,310
Three	1,114	1,107	1,247	1,217
Four to six	1,138	1,221	1,418	1,413
Seven to ten	352	420	515	444
Eleven and over	192	202	281	346
Total firms	11,289	10,440	10,654	9,614

Source: *Verkehrs-Wirtschaftliche Zahlen 1972* (Frankfurt: Bundesverband des Deutschen Güterfernverkehrs, 1973).

rest of the industry.[16] Tables WG–1 and WG–7 indicate that the percentage of firms with only one licensed vehicle has fallen from 52 percent of all firms with 23 percent of all vehicles in 1960 to 39 percent of all firms with 13 percent of all vehicles in 1970. At the same time, the proportion of firms with more than ten licensed vehicles more than doubled, from 1.7 percent of all firms to 3.6 percent of all firms. The proportion of licensed vehicles owned by these large firms went from 11.7 percent to 21.3 percent. Thus, while the industry is still more or less unconcentrated, there seems to have been a definite trend toward larger firms. In spite of the fact that the number of firms has declined and that the total number of licensed trucks has risen at an annual rate of less than 1.4 percent, the number of large firms has increased at an annual rate of about 6 percent and the number of their vehicles licensed for long-distance operations has risen at an annual rate of 7.6 percent. Nevertheless, the four largest firms had only 1.5 percent of all employees (Table WG–8). The largest number of licenses held by one firm is only 102 and the largest four firms have among them only 352 licenses out of the total of 29,487. The largest cooperative has 1,200

[16] Interview with Mr. Binbrook of the Bundesverband des Deutschen Güterfernverkehrs, Frankfurt, November 1973; see also Table WG-7.

Table WG–8
PROFESSIONAL ROAD HAULAGE FIRMS: EMPLOYEE SIZE, 1970

Number of Employees in Firm	Number of Firms	Total Number of Employees	Percentage of All Firms	Percentage of All Employees
1	26,261	26,261	40.6	8.4
2 to 4	25,503	65,984	39.4	21.3
5 to 9	7,985	51,187	1.2	16.5
10 to 19	3,122	40,744	4.8	13.2
20 to 49	1,277	36,721	2.0	11.9
50 to 99	268	18,355	0.4	5.9
100 to 199	137	18,365	0.2	5.9
200 to 499	101	31,131	0.2	10.1
500 to 999	24	16,418	0.04	5.3
1,000 or more	4	4,511	0.006	1.5
Total	64,682	309,677		

Source: *Statistisches Jahrbuch* 1973. Statistisches Bundesamt, Wiesbaden, W. Kohlhammer GMBH, Stuttgart, pp. 190-91.

vehicles with 20,000 employees and takes in about 300,000,000 DM revenue each year.[17] This would mean that this one group had about 2.7 percent of all the vehicles used in professional long-distance transport, 6.5 percent of all the employees in long-distance transport, and took in about 8.2 percent of the revenues—by most standards that industry is still extremely unconcentrated and potentially highly competitive.

The actual degree of concentration is much higher than these data would indicate. The German road haulage trade association has fostered cooperatives among the smaller firms.[18] There are at least twenty such major cooperatives which in turn belong to one large cooperative.[19] Moreover, in actual practice many of the firms with only one or two licensed vehicles may not operate independently or even

---

[17] Data provided in the Binbrook interview and in a letter from Mr. Renfordt of the Bundesanstalt für den Güterfernverkehr, Cologne.
[18] Bundesverband des Deutschen Güterfernverkehrs, ["Organization, Tasks, and Development of the Commercial Long-Distance Goods Transport in the Federal Republic of Germany,"] mimeographed (Frankfurt), p. 13.
[19] Ibid., p. 12.

in a cooperative. To an unknown extent many charter themselves and their vehicle or vehicles to a larger haulage firm on a long-term basis. While nominally they are independent entrepreneurs, in practice they are in effect employees of a larger enterprise. As can be seen from Table WG–7, the number of firms with only one or two vehicles has declined, implying that these very small firms are not economically efficient.

Of course, many firms specialize in handling only one kind or a few kinds of traffic. About one-quarter of the trucks used in long-distance transport are specialized in some way. Most firms, even though authorized to carry anywhere in West Germany, limit the territory within which they operate.

In sum, concentration is considerably higher than the raw statistics would indicate and appears to have been increasing. The growth of the large firms and the development of cooperatives indicate that for long-distance transportation the smallest firm is not as viable as are firms of somewhat larger size. In other words, there are some economies of scale, at least within the strictly regulated industry. It would appear that the minimum economically efficient size is a firm with at least two vehicles.

The original main objective of regulation was to protect the railroads from competition from road haulage. To accomplish this, road haulage rates were tied to railroad rates until 1961. Trucking capacity has been limited and over-the-road transport has been subject to heavy taxation. At one time the government even planned to ban the carriage of certain kinds of commodities by road. However there was such a protest by shippers and truckers that this plan was not implemented.[20]

Notwithstanding the efforts on their behalf, the railroads have continued to lose market share to road haulage. In 1950 railroads carried 86 percent of the tons moved by rail or long-distance truck. By 1960 the figure had shrunk to 76 percent, by 1970 to 70 percent, and by 1972 to only 65 percent.[21] In ton-miles in 1950 the railroads had 62 percent of the long-distance traffic moved by rail, road, and inland waterway, while the long-distance road haulage industry (including own-account) moved only 11 percent. By 1967 the rail share had fallen to just over 40 percent while the road share had grown to over 25 percent.

[20] Interview with Dr. Pusch, Ministry of Transport, 22 November 1973.
[21] Derived from figures in Table WG-3.

In 1972 31 percent of the ton-miles was moved by road and only 41 percent by rail.

It must be acknowledged, however, that the percentage of traffic moving by rail is generally higher in West Germany than it is in most developed countries. Transport distances are longer in West Germany than they are in most other European countries, and this means that the rails have a natural advantage for carrying a higher proportion of goods in West Germany than elsewhere in Europe. Even so, it must be remembered that the losses of the West German federal railroad have recently reached extremely high levels.

The factors that explain the railroad's overall loss in market share and poor economic performance are its loss in traffic to trucks—and in part to water carriers—and a decrease in overall tonnage shipped for some commodities. Table WG–9 gives the tons carried by the various modes of transport from 1950 to 1972 (by major commodity group), and Table WG–10 shows the relative market shares of railroads and trucks. The railroads have actually increased their market share of coal tonnage, but since the total shipment of coal has declined during the postwar period, and especially since 1960, the total tonnage moved by rail in 1972 was about the same as it was in 1950 and about 23 percent less than it was in 1960. Because coal represented 40 percent of the tonnage carried by railroad in 1950, this loss has been telling.

On the other hand, rail has lost to road haulage its preeminent market share of vehicles, machines, and other manufactured goods carried. Road haulage competed for the transport of these goods because they are the most profitable to carry. The railroad has also lost in its market share of chemical products. The net result can be seen in Table WG–11. Since 1955, the revenues of West German railroads have increased 116 percent, but the revenue of long-distance road haulage firms has increased 242 percent. In real terms, rail revenues increased 33 percent but long-distance trucking revenues increased 110 percent.

The special tax levied on road haulage at the beginning of 1969 combined with the extra levy on own-account road haulage did have a noticeable effect. Own-account trucking had carried nearly 21 percent of the ton-miles moved by road in 1968, and this proportion fell to less than 18 percent in 1970.[22] At the same time the proportion of t⸱ n-miles

----
[22] Ibid.

Table WG–9

MAJOR COMMODITIES BY TRANSPORT MODE,
SELECTED YEARS, 1950–72

(millions of metric tons)

	1950	1960	1965	1970	1972
Professional long-distance road transport					
Land and forest products	2.5	6.5	5.9	5.8	5.8
Food and fodder	3.5	8.5	11.7	13.8	15.4
Coal	0.4	1.3	0.8	0.5	0.4
Crude oil	0	0.2	0	0	0
Refined petroleum products	0.1	4.1	6.1	6.6	6.3
Metal ores and scrap metal	0.3	0.5	0.6	0.7	0.7
Iron, steel, and nonprecious metals	2.7	9.0	9.3	10.2	9.6
Stone, cement, and soil	4.4	19.4	21.8	19.6	20.8
Fertilizer	0	0.1	0.1	0.2	0.5
Chemical products	0.9	3.5	5.7	9.0	10.5
Vehicles, machines, and other manufactured goods	4.8	18.2	26.4	38.3	42.3
Total	19.6	71.3	88.4	104.8	112.3
Own-account					
Land and forest products	1.8	3.1	3.3	3.9	4.8
Food and fodder	2.8	7.2	10.4	12.4	14.5
Coal	0.5	0.3	0.3	0.1	0.2
Crude oil	0	0	0	0	0
Refined petroleum products	0.3	1.1	1.5	1.5	3.0
Metal ores and scrap metal	0.1	0.2	0.3	0.3	0.3
Iron, steel, and nonprecious metals	0.5	1.4	1.8	2.1	2.5
Stone, cement, and soil	4.8	2.2	3.5	3.6	7.9
Fertilizer	0.1	0.1	0.1	0.1	0.1
Chemical products	0.3	0.8	1.5	2.2	2.6
Vehicles, machines, and other manufactured goods	2.1	7.1	11.4	14.9	17.1
Total	13.3	23.5	34.1	41.1	53.0

Table WG–9 (continued)

	1950	1960	1965	1970	1972
Railroads					
Land and forestry products	18.6	22.5	22.5	24.7	23.2
Food and fodder	4.2	5.2	6.4	8.6	8.2
Coal	83.7	106.9	94.4	95.4	82.3
Crude oil	2.1	3.8	2.8	2.0	1.9
Refined petroleum products	4.5	10.5	19.0	28.8	30.7
Metal ores and scrap metal	18.8	46.9	40.4	54.1	48.0
Iron, steel, and nonprecious metals	13.7	32.6	36.0	57.0	55.3
Stone, cement, and soil	32.0	39.0	36.1	38.7	35.9
Fertilizer	7.6	14.1	15.1	16.8	15.8
Chemical products	5.9	11.8	14.7	18.4	18.5
Vehicles, machines, and other manufactured goods	17.7	22.3	29.0	33.5	33.8
Total	208.8	315.7	311.4	378.0	353.0
Water carriers					
Land and forestry products	4.2	8.0	7.4	9.1	7.8
Food and fodder	2.1	4.8	5.7	6.9	7.7
Coal	25.9	37.6	28.1	24.6	18.9
Crude oil	0.9	3.5	2.5	1.3	1.1
Refined petroleum products	2.5	17.3	29.5	40.3	41.8
Metal ores and scrap metal	9.6	30.9	30.1	37.5	33.1
Iron, steel, and nonprecious metals	3.1	9.2	11.3	14.8	14.5
Stone, cement, and soil	19.1	49.2	66.5	87.5	84.9
Fertilizer	2.1	5.4	6.5	6.2	5.8
Chemical products	1.7	4.6	6.6	10.1	10.7
Vehicles, machines, and other manufactured goods	0.7	1.5	1.5	1.7	2.2
Total	71.9	172.0	195.7	240.0	228.5

Source: West Germany, Ministry of Transport, *Verkehr in Zahlen 1973* (Bonn, 1973).

Table WG–10

RAILROAD AND LONG-DISTANCE ROAD SHARES OF MARKET FOR SELECTED MAJOR PRODUCT CLASSES, SELECTED YEARS, 1950–72

Product Class	1950	1960	1965	1970	1972
Land and forest products					
Railroads	68.6	56.1	57.5	56.8	55.8
Road	15.9	23.9	23.5	22.3	25.5
Food and fodder					
Railroads	33.3	20.2	18.7	20.6	17.9
Road	50.0	63.0	64.6	62.8	65.3
Coal					
Railroads	75.7	73.2	76.4	79.1	80.8
Road	0.8	1.1	0.9	0.5	0.6
Refined petroleum products					
Railroads	60.8	31.8	33.9	37.3	37.5
Road	4.1	15.8	13.5	10.5	11.4
Metal ores and scrap metal					
Railroads	65.3	59.7	56.6	58.4	58.5
Road	1.4	0.9	1.3	1.1	1.2
Iron, steel, and nonprecious metals					
Railroads	68.5	62.5	61.6	67.8	67.5
Road	16.0	19.9	19.0	14.6	14.7
Stone, cement, and soil					
Railroads	53.1	35.5	28.2	25.9	24.0
Road	15.3	19.6	19.8	15.5	19.2
Chemical products					
Railroads	67.0	57.0	51.6	46.3	43.7
Road	13.0	20.8	25.3	28.2	31.0
Fertilizers					
Railroads	77.6	71.6	69.3	72.1	71.2
Road	1.0	1.0	0.9	1.3	2.7
Vehicles, machines, and other manufactured goods					
Railroads	70.0	45.4	42.5	37.9	35.2
Road	27.3	51.5	55.3	60.2	61.9

Source: West Germany, Ministry of Transport, *Verkehr in Zahlen 1973* (Bonn, 1973).

Table WG–11

PROFESSIONAL TRANSPORT FREIGHT REVENUES, SELECTED YEARS, 1955–72

(millions of DMs)

	Railroads			Inland Waterways	Long-Distance Road Haulage[a]	Total
Year	Government	Other	Total			
1955	3,912	156	4,068	820	1,235	6,123
1960	5,113	223	5,336	1,100	2,027	8,463
1965	5,442	202	5,644	1,220	2,638	9,502
1966	5,577	200	5,777	1,240	2,776	9,793
1967	5,257	200	5,457	1,360	2,734	9,551
1968	5,932	210	6,142	1,580	3,015	10,737
1969	6,724	224	6,948	1,860	3,314	12,122
1970	7,544	255	7,799	2,060	3,649	13,508
1971	8,130	266	8,396	2,100	4,087	14,583
1972	8,510	282	8,792	2,150	4,226	15,168

[a] Excluding value-added tax.

Source: Data from *Verkehr in Zahlen 1973,* tables B54, B55, B60; *Verkehrs-Wirtschaftliche Zahlen 1972;* and the Joint Statistical Report of the Federal Institute for Long-Distance Road Transport (Cologne) and the Federal Office for Motoring (Flensburg).

moved by road fell from 26.1 percent the year before the tax to 25.7 the year after. Actually, the decline in the share carried by road is attributable entirely to the decrease in traffic moved by own-account trucking. The railroads apparently did benefit from the tax, because the percentage of ton-miles carried by rail increased from 40.8 to 43.6 the year after the tax was in effect and to 44.1 in 1970. Since the removal of the tax at the end of 1971, the proportion of ton-miles moved by own-account trucking has returned to a level close to 20 percent and own-account trucking is apparently growing more rapidly than professional trucking. This fact suggests that some shippers are unhappy with professional trucking, perhaps because of excessive rates and inadequate service.

Although regulation may have stabilized the industry, it has also built monopoly gains into the road-haulage industry, as may be seen by the large sums spent for licenses. Nevertheless, as Table WG–12 shows, there has been a surprisingly large number of bankruptcies among those

Table WG–12

NUMBER OF BANKRUPTCIES, EXITS, AND ENTRIES FOR JOINT STOCK AND LIMITED LIABILITY ROAD TRANSPORT COMPANIES, 1967–72

Year	Number of Firms	Bank-ruptcies	Other Exits	Total Exits	Entries
1967	616	10	11	21	94
1968	670	15	11	26	78
1969	737	11	12	23	98
1970	817	17	20	37	118
1971	880	14	25	37	107
1972	957	26	25	51	129

Source: *Statistisches Jahrbuch* 1968–1973, Statistisches Bundesamt, Wiesbaden, W. Kohlhammer GMBH, Stuttgart, pp. 190–91.

few road haulage firms which are joint stock and limited liability companies. Given the high value of a license, it would be reasonable to expect few if any bankruptcies, since in many cases it should be possible to sell licenses to cover debts. Short-distance transport, which is much less stringently regulated, is more profitable than long-distance transport (Table WG–5). Rates appear to be quite stable in short-distance transport even with the large movement permitted within the margin and despite the fact that the rates are not really policed. Of course, rates in long-distance traffic are also stable, though whether this is inherent in the market or the result of regulation cannot be determined without going beyond the West German experience.

Conclusion

Regulation in West Germany has attempted to protect the railroads from truck competition, but it has failed despite restrictions on the growth of trucking. Regulation has fostered high rates (which are at least 11 percent higher than they would otherwise be) and created monopoly gains for the possessors of licenses. Monopoly profits have not led truckers to subsidize unprofitable service from profitable traffic. They have preferred to concentrate on the profitable traffic, with the result that service quality to some areas is reported to be inadequate. Apparently rates to these areas are not high enough to attract trucking.

3
Regulation in Belgium

Outside of Great Britain, the European trucking industry is least regulated in Belgium. Capacity control is slight and tariff control exists for only a few commodities and for international traffic. This was not always the case.

During the 1930s the Belgian railroads suffered greatly from truck competition. After an abortive attempt to tax road transport for distances in excess of twenty kilometers, the government proposed legislation to license professional road haulage in order "to bring a better coordination of transports by road and by rail." [1] The legislation was never enacted. However, a government decree of 5 March 1936 required the licensing of transport for hire and reward, while leaving own-account trucking entirely unregulated. The stated objectives were to keep capacity in road transport in balance with the needs of the traffic, to improve the quality of road transport companies, and to promote the coordination of the means of transport by preventing too-rapid growth. [2]

The 1936 decree divided road haulage for hire and reward into three categories. [3] The first category was not regulated but was confined to the transport of mail and parcel post, transport of human cadavers, occasional transport justified by an exceptional urgency, and transport by ordinary automobiles.

The second category was subject to the requirement that the operator get a certificate for the capacity of each vehicle from L'Office des Transports par Route (OTR). Transport within the boundaries of ports or within a radius of 10 kilometers of a firm's base (extended to

[1] *Lois et Règlements concernant le Transport Routier*, pt. 1: *Transport National* (Brussels: Institut du Transport Routier, 1973), p. 2.
[2] Ibid.
[3] Ibid., p. 4.

25 kilometers in 1951) fell into this category. There were no restrictions on the number of certificates or on the length of their validity. Thus there were never any controls on capacity in short-haul transportation.

The third category (all other haulage) was subject to the requirement that haulers secure licenses from the OTR. The 1936 decree required the OTR to consider the needs of traffic, together with technical improvements and the necessity of assuring the safety of transport. In practice the result was that it was virtually impossible for a new firm to secure a license, and extremely difficult for existing firms to expand. Need had to be proven for any increase in capacity and objections by the state railway were usually sufficient for the application to be denied. Transfer of a license was impossible, although a whole business could be sold.

While the system was modified slightly several times, it was nevertheless extremely rigid. By 1954 licenses generally were valid for the transport of all goods anywhere in Belgium. However, the OTR was authorized to issue licenses valid only for the transport of special goods, or for special regions, or for transport performed exclusively for one specified shipper or a few specified shippers.

By 1960 even professional haulers were frustrated with the system and wanted liberalization. Shippers and haulers both agreed on change. Also, in spite of regulation the Belgian railroad had, by this time, lost most of its domestic traffic to road haulage.

The law of 1 August 1960 greatly liberalized the system. It provided that any firm or person holding a national license would be granted additional licenses for as much additional capacity as requested, provided the firm's central office was situated in Belgium. Thus existing firms were allowed to increase their capacity immediately by as much as they desired. The law also provided that firms having local certificates for at least three years and grossing 40,000 Belgian francs (BF) (about $1,000) per ton of capacity per year, or 500,000 BF for a tractor for three years, be granted a national license for those vehicles having the certificates.

There are six categories of national licenses:

(1) for a vehicle with maximum capacity of not more than 2 tons;
(2) for a vehicle with maximum capacity of not more than 10 tons;
(3) for a vehicle with maximum capacity of not more than 15 tons;

(4) for a vehicle with capacity greater than 15 tons but which does not exceed 19 tons for a vehicle with two axles (semi-trailers excepted), or does not exceed 21 tons for a semi-trailer with one back axle, or does not exceed 28 tons for a semi-trailer with two or more back axles;

(5) for larger vehicles specially certified with the minister of communications;

(6) for tractors used to pull trailers.

When a certificate is exchanged for a national license the firm making the exchange is allowed to increase the capacity of each vehicle by one size category. Two years after receiving the authorization, if the firm can show that it took in annually 40,000 BF per ton of capacity, it may increase the capacity one more category. Six years after a firm has received national licenses for its vehicles, it may apply for an unlimited number of licenses of any capacity if it can show that during the six years its vehicles took in at least 40,000 BF annually per ton of licensed capacity.

The transfer of national licenses is permitted under restricted conditions. A transfer can be made with full rights of the licenses or without the rights. The rights referred to are those relating to the ability to secure unlimited licenses after six years of national operation. If the licenses are transferred without rights, the operator acquiring the license must operate for six years grossing 40,000 BF per year per ton before he can expand his operations.

A transfer with rights can be made to the license-holder's spouse, son, daughter, or relative up to the second degree. It can also be made to a partnership or company if the original holder subscribes half the capital for three years and during that period actively operates within the management of the company, or to an individual who for six years has participated in the active management of the license-holder's company. A transfer without rights can be made to one or more persons who have participated for six years in the management of the transport company or to a company or an individual without the requisite six years of experience. In the latter case the original owner must subscribe half the capital of the new enterprise for three years.

To secure a certificate to operate in short-distance transport, an applicant must submit evidence of domicile, nationality, and good morals. For the vehicle, evidence must be submitted showing the technical characteristics of the truck, trailer, semi-trailer, or tractor—that is, the registration number of chassis, the kind of vehicle, the unladen weight, the capacity, and the dimensions of the vehicle. After that a certificate will be issued for the vehicle to operate within a 25-kilometer radius of the firm's head office or of a specific branch office. In effect, then, there is no limitation on entry into the short-haul market.

A firm possessing a certificate may haul goods for any shipper anywhere within 25 kilometers of its base, whereas a firm with a general license may haul goods anywhere within Belgium or Luxembourg. For all goods except those coming under the European Coal and Steel Community Treaty—coal, coke, iron, iron ore, scrap iron, steel, and so on—there are no controls on rates charged. For products coming under the treaty, a basic rate has been established by the government, but truckers may deviate up or down by 15 percent from this rate. Until recently actual rates tended to be at the bottom of the bracket, but government officials have said that in the winter of 1974 fuel price increases caused rates to move close to the top and firms were asking for a 20 percent rise.[4]

Because of Belgium's small size, international traffic, outside of the Benelux area, is important. A firm must have an international license in order to operate in international haulage and, for most countries, it needs bilateral or multilateral authorizations as well. To secure an international license a firm must have a general national license for the vehicle it proposes to use in international haulage. In addition the firm must have someone in "daily administration" who has a certificate of professional competency.

Securing a certificate of professional competency is difficult, and less than 50 percent of the applicants succeed in doing so each year.[5] To earn this certificate it is necessary to pass an examination given by the Institut du Transport Routier (ITR, the Institute of Road Transport) on national and international haulage. Generally the applicant takes a written examination on specified topics in September. If successful, he then takes an oral examination on the remainder of the required topics. Some of the topics upon which an applicant is examined are the practical elements of accounting, the current exchange of commercial letters,

[4] Interview with M. de Borger, Ministère des Communications et des Postes, Télégraphes et Téléphones, Administration des Transports, February 1974.
[5] Interview with Mlle. De Hert, Fédération Nationale Belge des Transporteurs Routiers, February 1974.

and the determination of the cost price and of the transport price. The ITR offers a course for those intending to take the examination. If an applicant fails, he may repeat the examination until he passes it.[6]

An individual who has a certificate of professional competency is permitted to be in the "daily administration" of no more than two firms. Legally he is meant to be actively involved in the firm's operations, but in practice there are cases where a person is paid for the use of his name but does not take an active interest in the firm. If a firm loses the person with the certificate it has one year in which to secure another person so qualified—or in the event of death of the person with the certificate, up to two years.[7]

A firm with an international license is in a position to request a bilateral or multilateral authorization if it can show that it has shippers desiring to have their goods carried to the particular countries involved. Since such authorizations, especially the multilateral ones, are limited in number, a new firm is generally granted only a few authorizations until it shows that it can efficiently use more.[8]

For international trade with the original six members of the Common Market, there are bilateral tariff agreements which the hauler is supposed to follow. These prescribe rates for various classifications of commodities, and the hauler is allowed to reduce rates below the legal maximum by as much as 23 percent. Table B–1 gives some typical rates for two of the four classes. In general, Class I includes specialty goods moving at premium rates; Class II, normal goods; Class III, low-valued goods; and Class IV, bulk low-valued goods moving at the lowest rates.[9] Figure B–1 shows what the rates actually were for the first six months of 1972 in comparison with the legal rates.

In addition, haulers are permitted to negotiate special tariffs outside the limits of the brackets when there are special circumstances involved, when the tonnage to be carried under such a contract within any three-month period is 500 metric tons or more, and when the contract will maintain or increase the carrier's profits. Small discounts are also per-

---

[6] Ibid.

[7] *Lois et Règlements concernant le Transport Routier*, pt. 2: *Transport International* (Brussels: Institut du Transport Routier, 1973), p. 12.

[8] Interview with M. Dirckx, director of commercial service for Transport Coulier, Brussels, 28 January 1974.

[9] See *Extrait du "Moniteur Belge,"* 6 October 1971, for a detailed list of products and their classification.

Table B–1
TYPICAL BILATERAL TARIFFS
(Belgian francs per metric ton)

Distance		Within Benelux				To and from West Germany			
		10 tons		20 tons		10 tons		20 tons	
Kms	Miles	Class I	Class IV	Class I	Class IV	Class I	Class IV	Class I	Class IV
50	31	none	none	none	none	none	none	none	none
81	50	267	222	187	157	392	287	279	205
100	62	293	246	207	173	429	316	305	224
161	100	426	357	300	251	594	436	422	309
323	200	734	615	517	433	1,015	745	723	530
800	497	1,593	1,334	1,122	939	1,847	1,355	1,316	965

Note: These are maximum rates; actual rates can be as much as 23 percent lower. In addition, under special circumstances, special contracts can be negotiated for even lower rates.

Source: Data from the bilateral agreement between Belgium and West Germany (printed in the *Extrait du "Moniteur Belge,"* 6 October 1971) and the Benelux agreement (Décision du Comité de Ministres de l'Union Economique Benelux en Matière de Transports de Merchandise par Route, M[71]19, 4 May 1971).

Figure B–1

COMPARISON OF ACTUAL RATES AND LEGAL BRACKET RATES,
BELGIAN CARRIERS, FIRST HALF OF 1972

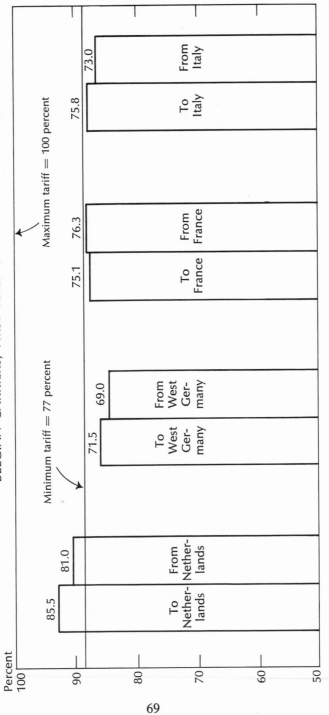

Source: Ministère des Communications et des Postes, Télégraphes et Téléphones, Administration des Transports, Direction C1, "Annual Report for 1972," mimeographed.

mitted when intermediaries such as agents and freight forwarders are used.[10]

The Results of the System

Freight transport in Belgium is carried predominantly by road (see Table B–2). In 1972 trucks carried 67 percent of freight tonnage, inland water carriers handled 19 percent, and railroads handled 14 percent. In terms of ton-miles, the railroad had a somewhat larger share of the market—25 percent. Railroads have been losing their share of the market to motor carriers. In the ten years from 1963 to 1972, the railroads lost 6.4 percentage points and truckers gained about 7.1 percentage points. The rapidly growing share of the market held by the trucking industry suggests that trucking is performing well in comparison with the state railway.

Even though there is no control over rates in Belgium and little control over entry, rates appear to be stable. One major user reported that his firm has periodically called for bids and, within limits, took those who offered the best price and appeared to be likely to give the best service. Until the oil shortage created huge increases in diesel fuel prices, most freight rates had declined over four or five years, after adjustment was made for inflation. Money rates were often identical for one or two years (see Table B–3).

Figure B–1 shows that, for the first six months of 1972, international rates tended to be around or below the minimum margin. One trucking firm [11] claimed that it could get rates above the maximum permitted tariff because of the specialized nature of its work. There were also reports of collusion in rate setting in some segments of the market.[12] However, with easy entry and no requirement to publish rates for domestic transport (except for coal and steel products), collusion would seem unlikely to be very effective.

Data on profits are fragmentary. Industry spokesmen have said that profits are generally less than 10 percent of revenue.[13] One of the

---

[10] See any of the international agreements between Belgium and other Common Market countries as for example the Belgian-West German agreement printed in the *Extrait du "Moniteur Belge,"* 6 October 1971.

[11] A large Belgian hauler of dangerous liquids.

[12] Ibid.

[13] Interview with J. Van Stappen, director of the Institut du Transport Routier, February 1974.

Table B–2

FREIGHT TRAFFIC IN BELGIUM, BY MODE, 1963–72
(including imports and exports)

Year	Railroad	Road Haulage	Inland Water	Total
		Millions of Metric Tons		
1963	65.9	195.1	64.8	327.7
1964	67.2	—	76.3	—
1965	64.5	225.6	77.0	368.1
1966	59.9	233.2	79.6	372.8
1967	60.0	243.7	85.3	389.0
1968	63.8	248.0	93.3	405.2
1969	69.8	265.7	92.7	428.2
1970	71.8	315.3	91.6	478.6
1971	67.0	342.1	95.4	504.5
1972	69.9	338.9	96.4	505.2
		Billions of Ton-Kilometers		
1963	6.9	6.6	5.2	18.7
1964	7.0	—	6.1	—
1965	6.8	8.5	6.1	21.4
1966	6.3	9.6	6.0	21.9
1967	6.1	10.0	6.3	22.4
1968	6.7	10.6	6.7	23.9
1969	7.5	11.6	6.9	26.0
1970	7.9	13.1	6.7	27.7
1971	7.4	14.3	6.7	28.4
1972	7.5	15.2	6.8	29.5

Source: Ministère des Communications et des Postes, Télégraphes et Téléphones, *Les Transports en Belgique, Recueil de Statistiques,* 9th ed. (Brussels, 1974).

larger and more profitable trucking companies reported that its profits in the last year had been nearly 12 percent of revenue.[14] Table B–4 indicates that in only one out of three recent years did the sample of incorporated transport companies (including bus and taxi companies) earn a profit as a whole.

---

[14] Interview with Dirckx.

Table B–3

TYPICAL TRUCKING RATES WITHIN BELGIUM, 1969–74
(Belgian francs per metric ton-kilometer)

Year	Bulk Liquid (22-ton load)	Bulk Powder in Hopper Trucks (24-ton load)	Manufactured Package Product (10-ton load)
1969		1.04	0.80
1970	1.62	1.11	0.90
1971	1.62	1.19	0.95
1972	1.85	1.00	1.00
1973	1.85	1.08	1.10
1974	2.15	1.19	1.25

Source: Confidential report of a large American company.

Data provided by the Ministry of Communications indicate that in 1973 there were 213 enterprises granted new national licenses, about 2.7 percent of the total number of enterprises holding national licenses. There were 361 enterprises holding national licenses that left the industry—4.6 percent of the total—but the number of licensed vehicles rose from 40,983 at the end of 1972 to 43,338 at the end of 1973. The 213 firms that graduated from holding certificates to holding national licenses were 5.4 percent of those with certificates.[15]

Would-be truckers are often willing to pay a premium to avoid having to wait nine years to earn a national license. While it is difficult to purchase a license with full rights, apparently it is done. The going price reported to me was about 300,000 to 350,000 BF or about $7,500 to $8,500 for an unlimited license.[16] To buy a license it is necessary that the original owner appear to be half-owner of the new enterprise and appear to participate in the management of the firm.

Apparently it is not easy for firms to earn the 40,000 BF per ton of capacity required in order to qualify for a national license. If a firm asks for a certificate for a truck with small capacity in order to make it easy to earn the necessary revenue in short-distance haulage, its capacity

[15] Letter from P. Cattrysse of the secretariat, general office of the Ministère des Communications et des Postes, Télégraphes et Téléphones, Brussels, 22 March 1974.

[16] Interview with Dirckx.

Table B–4

PROFITS AND LOSSES OF INCORPORATED BELGIAN ROAD TRANSPORT COMPANIES, 1968–70

	1968	1969	1970
Total number of companies	162	174	193
Total capital	434,764	483,552	562,588
Total retained earnings	272,482	243,685	300,535
Net profits	—10,655	—10,423	70,964
Rate of return on capital and retained earnings	—1.5%	—1.4%	8.2%
Profitable firms	111	118	154
Capital	310,673	330,268	454,224
Retained earnings	194,745	210,107	271,515
Profits	44,880	55,887	108,316
Rate of return on capital and retained earnings	8.9%	11.1%	14.9%
Avg. size in terms of capital and retained earnings	$108,412	$109,236	$112,205
Unprofitable firms	51	56	39
Capital	124,091	153,254	108,364
Retained earnings	77,737	33,578	29,020
Profits	—55,535	—69,310	—37,352
Avg. size in terms of capital and retained earnings	$ 94,224	$ 79,435	$ 83,873

Note: Unless otherwise indicated, financial data are in thousands of Belgian francs. Forty Belgian francs equal $1.00.
Source: Ministère des Affaires Economiques, Institut National de Statistique, *Statistiques Financières 1973*, no. 2.

will be too limited for adequate use to be made of the national license when the firm receives a national license three years later—though the firm can upgrade the capacities of its vehicles by one category. On the other hand, a vehicle with large capacity is hard to use efficiently in short-distance transport. It is, however, important to note that a firm properly located near Brussels can serve 60 percent of Belgian traffic with a short-distance license.

Some statistics furnished by the Ministry of Communications indicate that most firms with local certificates have difficulty qualifying for national licenses.[17] On average, in any year at least one-quarter of the firms with certificates would have met the time requirement for qualifying for a national license during that year. Since many firms do not meet the revenue requirement, more than one-quarter of the firms with certificates must have had certificates for three years. If only one-quarter met the time requirements during 1973, there would have been 993 firms ready to qualify for national licenses. However, only 213 (or about 21 percent of 993) in fact received national licenses. Actually there must be fewer than 21 percent earning 40,000 BF per ton of capacity, because the number of firms having held certificates for three years is undoubtedly higher than 993.

According to data provided by the Ministry of Communications, roughly 920 firms with local certificates left the industry in 1973.[18] Since 213 received national licenses, there was a gross reduction of 1,133 firms with certificates. The number of firms with local certificates fell by 469, so that 664 firms must have received new local certificates. If this is typical of the rate of entry in previous years, we can calculate that at the start of 1973 there would have been 1,980 firms which had met the time requirement. During 1973 an additional 664 firms would have met the time requirement, so that by the end of 1973 a total of 2,644 firms would have operated three or more years. Only 8 percent of this number apparently met the revenue requirements to qualify for a national license. We can reasonably conclude that between 8 percent and 21 percent of the firms with local certificates were able to meet the revenue requirements in 1973. The 40,000 BF per ton capacity requirement was originally established in 1960; entry must have been considerably more difficult at that time than it is currently, because price levels have increased approximately 50 percent since then.

Thus, inflation is making it easier than it has been in the past for firms to meet the fixed revenue requirements. Partly as a consequence of this, the industry has been pushing for some change in the law.[19] Discussion has centered around increasing the revenue requirement of 700,000 BF (about $17,500) irrespective of capacity, introducing a competency examination for those wishing to have a local certificate,

---

[17] Letter from Cattrysse.
[18] Ibid.
[19] Interview with De Hert.

and setting up a more difficult examination than is now given for those wanting a national license.[20] No action has been taken on these proposals.

Although a fairly large number of firms leaves the industry each year—in 1973 a total of 1,281 firms out of 11,863 [21]—only a few firms actually go into bankruptcy. In 1971, the only year for which data are available, there were thirty-eight failures of firms in professional transport—both freight and passenger—out of the total of 11,892 road haulage firms plus an unknown number of taxi firms.[22]

While profits do not appear to be high in Belgium and rates generally appear to be low relative to costs, service quality appears to be good. Shippers report no complaints about service.[23] Transport is efficient, prompt, and available to any place.

From Table B–5 it can be seen that own-account trucking holds a substantial share of domestic road transport. Professional transport may have gained slightly in relation to own-account, but there does not seem to have been much change in recent years. The small share of traffic carried by professional transport is largely explained by the short distances involved in domestic transport within such a small country as Belgium. As can be seen from Table B–6, in 1971 the mean "long-distance" trip was 61.5 miles for own-account transport and only 64.7 miles for professional transport. This figure for "long-distance" haulage excludes all haulage under 50 kilometers (about 31 miles).

For international transport, haulage distances are considerably greater and consequently professional transport has a larger share of the market. Private trucking is most economical in short-distance haulage where empty backhauls are not as costly. Table B–5 shows that professional transport carries about two-thirds of the international tons and about 70 percent of the ton-miles that go by road. There do not seem to have been any significant changes in the proportion of goods going by own-account over the years 1963–72.

It should be noted that professional transportation tends to be more efficient than own-account transportation: own-account firms have 88 percent of the vehicles and 67 percent of the capacity, but carry

[20] Interview with Van Stappen.

[21] Letter from Cattrysse.

[22] *L'Avenir du Transport Routier*, no. 1052 (6 April 1972), p. 6.

[23] Interview with M. Delsaux, Fédération des Enterprises de Belgique, January 1974.

Table B–5
DOMESTIC AND INTERNATIONAL ROAD HAULAGE
BY BELGIAN FIRMS, 1963–72

	Millions of Metric Tons			Millions of Ton-Kilometers		
Year	Own-account	Profes-sional	Percent-age profes-sional	Own-account	Profes-sional	Percent-age profes-sional
Domestic Haulage						
1963	124.1	63.5	33.8	3.3	2.0	37.9
1964	—	—	—	—	—	—
1965	139.7	76.8	35.5	4.1	2.3	36.3
1966	151.1	70.1	31.7	4.6	2.5	35.2
1967	157.5	74.2	32.0	4.7	2.5	34.7
1968	156.7	77.6	33.1	4.7	2.7	36.4
1969	164.5	84.9	34.0	4.9	3.0	38.0
1970	196.0	101.8	34.0	5.6	3.6	39.1
1971	212.8	111.6	34.4	6.0	3.9	39.3
1972	208.9	110.1	34.5	5.9	4.2	41.3
International Haulage						
1963	2.3	5.2	69.7	299	976	76.5
1964	—	—	—	—	—	—
1965	3.6	6.6	64.9	605	1,480	71.0
1966	4.2	7.8	64.7	779	1,789	69.7
1967	4.2	7.9	65.3	794	2,006	71.6
1968	4.8	9.5	66.4	897	2,321	72.1
1969	6.0	10.4	63.5	1,182	2,515	68.0
1970	6.1	10.4	62.8	1,264	2,629	67.5
1971	6.6	11.1	62.6	1,530	2,897	65.4
1972	6.8	13.1	65.8	1,531	3,570	70.0

Source: Ministère des Communications et des Postes, Télégraphes et Téléphones, *Les Transports en Belgique, Recueil de Statistiques,* 9th ed. (Brussels, 1974).

only 49 percent of the ton-miles. In addition, a spokesman for the ITR reported to me that the rate of utilization of vehicles in professional haulage was 44 percent domestically and 52 percent in international transport, but the rate of utilization in own-account haulage was only

Table B-6

BELGIAN ROAD TRANSPORT DISTANCES, 1971

(millions of tons)

Distance	Domestic Transport	International Transport	Domestic Ordinary Transport		International Ordinary Transport	
			Own-account	Professional	Own-account	Professional
0 to 24 km	202.7	0.4	12.1	3.8	0.1	0.1
25 to 49 km	52.6	1.7	9.0	4.2	0.2	0.3
50 to 99 km	44.8	2.8	10.4	8.4	0.6	0.8
100 to 199 km	22.0	4.5	7.0	7.2	1.4	2.4
200 and over	2.3	8.3	0.7	0.8	2.6	5.2
Total	324.4	17.7	39.8	24.4	4.9	8.7
Median kms (over 50 kms)	88.6	est. 212–216	93.4	98.7	230.7	248.3
Median miles (over 50 kms)	54.9	est. 131–134	57.9	61.2	143.0	153.0

Note: Ordinary road transport excludes distribution services and regular liner services (essentially parcels).
Source: Data from the Institut National de Statistique, *Statistiques des Transports 1972*, no. 12 (December 1972), pp. 58, 70–73.

40 percent and 43 percent, respectively.[24] The rate of utilization is defined as the ton-kilometers carried divided by the capacity of the vehicle in tons times the kilometers driven. It is of course affected by many factors, including the type of goods carried and the efficiency of the operations.

Concentration appears to be low in Belgium, although the data may be misleading. Table B–7 shows that in 1972 firms with twenty or more vehicles represented 4.6 percent of all firms with long-distance licenses and that these firms had about 42.5 percent of all the vehicles engaged in long-distance haulage. In 1967 firms with twenty or more vehicles represented only 2.2 percent of all firms and held only 26.6 percent of all vehicles. Evidently there was a tremendous increase in the number of firms in this category. All categories of size smaller than eleven vehicles per firm have shrunk in comparison to the total number of vehicles, so that there would appear to be economies of scale up to eleven vehicles per firm. Inasmuch as the number of smaller firms is shrinking absolutely there would appear to be marked economies of scale up to about five vehicles per firm.

As can be seen from Table B–7, in 1972 in the short-distance market 81 percent of the firms had only one vehicle, down from 87 percent in 1967. The proportion of firms with two vehicles increased, as did the proportion of firms in all categories—except for firms with six vehicles—up to the largest size. Apparently the minimum number of vehicles with which an entrant should expect to operate after becoming established is two.

In 1972 the 921 firms with 100 tons or more capacity (11.7 percent of all firms) had 32.5 percent of the total capacity and 61.6 percent of all vehicles (see Table B–8). In 1970, there were 753 firms with 100 tons or more capacity (9.5 percent of the firms). According to Ministry of Communication figures, the largest firm had 400 vehicles (including trailers and semi-trailers) and the largest four firms had 1,285 vehicles or 3.1 percent of the total number of vehicles.[25]

The relatively low concentration figures may be somewhat misleading. Many of the firms, including some of the largest, are owned by holding companies that own other haulage firms in other countries.[26]

---

[24] Interview with Van Stappen.

[25] Interview with De Borger.

[26] Interview with Guy Robberechts, director of Transport Creten, Brussels, 25 April 1974.

Table B-7

SIZE DISTRIBUTION OF BELGIAN ROAD HAULAGE FIRMS, 1967–72

Size of Fleet (number of vehicles)	Firms with All-Belgian Licenses						Firms with 25-Kilometer Certificates					
	1967	1968	1969	1970	1971	1972	1967	1968	1969	1970	1971	1972
One	4,642	4,277	4,185	4,115	4,004	3,920	3,093	3,284	3,290	3,114	3,331	3,227
Two	1,299	1,289	1,226	1,267	1,261	1,223	324	335	371	386	441	492
Three	537	530	525	513	501	503	68	76	90	95	94	115
Four	387	373	348	358	357	376	23	33	33	36	50	52
Five	256	236	292	290	290	304	11	8	22	20	22	24
Six	178	176	178	195	208	212	14	12	11	14	10	15
Seven	127	136	146	153	162	157	1	3	5	8	11	8
Eight to ten	255	262	279	319	334	363	7	7	12	19	20	19
Eleven to fifteen	173	208	242	274	272	281	6	7	6	7	9	10
Sixteen to twenty	93	110	110	143	174	187	4	3	—	3	3	6
Twenty or more	176	216	252	303	330	366	7	7	6	7	8	5
Total firms	8,123	7,813	7,733	7,930	7,893	7,892	3,558	3,775	3,846	3,709	3,999	3,973
Total vehicles	27,042	29,071	31,338	35,764	38,283	40,984	4,882	4,969	5,129	5,096	5,542	5,591

Note: Data compiled as of 31 December of each year.

Source: Ministère des Communications et des Postes, Télégraphes et Téléphones, Administration des Transports, Direction C1, annual reports for years shown, mimeographed.

Table B–8

NUMBER OF FIRMS IN BELGIAN ROAD HAULAGE, BY TOTAL AUTHORIZED CAPACITY, 1970–72

Year (as of 31 December)	Less than 5	5 to 10	10 to 15	15 to 20	20 to 25	25 to 50	50 to 100	100 or more
	Total Authorized Capacity in Metric Tons:							
---------------------- Firms with All-Belgian Licenses ----------------------								
1972	937	2,454	1,043	581	400	891	665	921
1971	984	2,561	1,050	545	408	871	648	827
1970	1,040	2,699	1,015	572	398	837	616	753
---------------------- Firms with 25-Kilometer Licenses ----------------------								
1972	1,261	1,658	431	254	118	184	45	22
1971	1,305	1,732	423	201	110	159	40	25
1970	1,273	1,629	376	182	82	107	45	15

Source: Ministère des Communications et des Postes, Télégraphes et Téléphones, Administration des Transports, Direction C1, annual reports for years shown, mimeographed.

Significant purchases of haulage firms by international companies have taken place in Belgium as well as in a number of other Common Market countries.[27]

In addition, the reported figure for very small firms with only one or two vehicles is misleading. Many of these firms are independent only in a legal sense. Often they work on a percentage basis for larger trucking enterprises on long-term contracts. I was told at one firm that in the past management had encouraged the employees to purchase a license and a vehicle and to work for the firm on a percentage basis. The former employees received a five-year contract under which they earned 72 percent on revenue for the first three years and 77 percent subsequently.[28] While statistically they were independent enterprises, in fact they were not. How large a proportion of the single-vehicle enterprises are not truly independent is unknown, but it must be substantial.

The result of this subcontracting is that the largest firms are in fact somewhat larger than the official statistics would indicate. For

---

[27] Ibid.; also interview with Dirckx.

[28] Interview with Dirckx.

Table B-9

SIZE OF BELGIAN ROAD HAULAGE FIRMS WITH COMMUNITY LICENSES, 31 DECEMBER 1970

Number of Vehicles	Number of Firms	Number of Employees	Number of Firms
1 to 4	7	—	—
5 to 9	23	less than 5	7
10 to 14	19	5 to 9	22
15 to 19	13	10 to 14	20
20 to 24	16	15 to 19	17
25 to 29	5	20 to 24	10
30 to 34	2	25 to 29	8
35 to 39	1	30 to 34	4
40 to 44	1	35 to 39	2
45 to 49	3	40 to 44	1
50 to 99	9	45 to 49	1
100 or more	6 [a]	50 or more	11 [b]
Total	2,951	105	2,188	103 [c]

[a] Largest six firms have about 30 percent of all vehicles.
[b] Largest eleven firms have about 35 percent of all employees
[c] Two firms did not provide data on number of employees.
Source: Ministère des Communications et des Postes, Télégraphes et Téléphones, *Echos des Communications,* no. 3 (1971).

example, one firm with 80 trucks of its own has 120 trucks and drivers under long-term contract along with 300 trailers which need no license.[29] The data on the size of Belgian firms with Community Licenses give a better idea of the concentration of business.[30] As can be seen from Table B-9, the largest category, with 100 or more vehicles, includes six firms. These make up about 6 percent of the total number of firms and have 30 percent of all vehicles. Even these data probably understate the concentration of international business, since there is undoubtedly some subcontracting in this area and some of these firms are undoubtedly owned by holding companies. Moreover, trucking firms tend to specialize both in the products they carry and in the areas they serve. Thus

---

[29] Ibid.
[30] A Community License permits the holder to carry goods from any one of the nine European Community countries to any other.

concentration may be substantial in many submarkets. One large trucker of cement claimed to have only five competitors—all of whom were friends.[31]

Conclusions

Before 1960 stringent regulation did not protect the railroads from highway competition, but it did inhibit professional trucking. The new system allows existing firms to expand without limit but restricts new entry to the short-distance market until the firm proves itself. Only a small number of short-distance truckers manage to earn enough to receive national licenses.

The result appears to be a highly competitive situation. Concentration may be high in some submarkets, but this apparently has not had anticompetitive consequences. There is no general control on prices, which are in fact freely negotiated. Rates are reasonable, profits modest, service quality good. The system allows for new entry or expansion in capacity with increases in demand. Firms are not large by comparison with firms in other countries, the largest being in the 300-to-400-vehicle classification. Concentration has increased, but that appears to have happened everywhere.

[31] Interview with Dirckx.

4

Regulation in the Netherlands

Prior to World War II there was no economic regulation of the trucking industry within the Netherlands. A proposal to institute regulation had been brought up in parliament just before the war started but had not been acted upon.

One reason the Dutch were late in instituting regulation was that there was little pressure for it from the railroads. The railroads had always faced active competition from water carriers and had never had a protected monopoly position. By 1939 a great deal of the freight business that had not been lost to the water carriers had been lost to road haulage, both professional and own-account.[1] Because of the short distances involved, trucks had a natural advantage over railroads for most goods.

Within a month after the Germans occupied the Netherlands they instituted a fixed-capacity limitation on the road haulage industry. No further expansion was permitted and, of course, with wartime shortages an actual decline in capacity took place. When the war ended the wartime restrictions were retained, but a government decree allowed all firms that had existed in 1939 to resume business and to expand capacity to the 1939 level.[2]

After parliament passed a new regulatory law in 1951 and before it went into effect in 1954 some further expansion in capacity took place. The 1951 act, which governs road haulage in the Netherlands today, established three basic kinds of professional trucking licenses: irregular, regular route, and pickup and delivery services. Each kind of

---

[1] Interview with Mr. Spoel of the Ministry of Transport, 22 April 1974.
[2] Ibid.

Table N–1

NUMBER AND CAPACITY OF PROFESSIONAL TRUCKING FIRMS, BY KIND OF LICENSE, 1 JANUARY 1972

Type of Carrier	Number of Firms	Capacity (thousands of tons)
Irregular route		
Unlimited	8,523	552.2
Limited	2,965	23.5
Regular route, scheduled service	973	27.4
International	1,197	109.3
Pickup and delivery	439	10.4
Total[a]	11,405	596.1

[a] Because some firms hold more than one type of license, the total number and capacity is not equal to the sum of the categories.

Source: Nationale Organisatie voor het Beroepsgoederenvervoer Wegtransport, *Wegvervoer in Cijfers 1973/74* (Rijswijk, Z. H., 1973).

license specifies the maximum capacity permitted the firm. Table N–1 gives the number of firms and the capacity permitted for each kind of licensed carrier. Own-account trucking is subject merely to registration—which has been refused only a few times in twenty years and those times only because the applicant was in fact engaged in for-hire trucking.[3]

Irregular trucking is the most important branch of the industry and includes 95.5 percent of the professional tonnage carried and 96.6 percent of the ton-kilometers driven (see Table N–2). An irregular license permits the holder to carry any goods for any customer anywhere within Holland and to perform international operations within the Benelux area. However, goods for no more than two shippers can be carried within the same truck at the same time.

Regular route truckers are licensed to carry goods only between specific points and are often limited in their authority to pick up goods at intermediate points. These firms have a common-carrier obligation and must offer regularly scheduled service, the frequency of which can

---

[3] Interview with Mr. van der Noordt of the Ministry of Transport, 2 April 1974.

Table N-2
INTERNAL FREIGHT TRAFFIC, BY MODE OF TRANSPORT, 1967–71

Mode of Transport	Millions of Metric Tons					Billions of Ton-Kilometers				
	1967	1968	1969	1970	1971	1967	1968	1969	1970	1971
Inland water	92.7	94.8	90.5	93.0	100.8	8.4	8.8	8.4	8.8	9.0
Railroad	14.0	12.7	12.0	11.5	9.2	2.0	1.8	1.7	1.7	1.5
Road haulage	268.7	276.4	297.0	304.5	309.7	10.2	11.1	11.7	12.4	13.1
Professional	154.5	163.3	173.5	180.9	190.2	6.5	7.3	7.8	8.4	8.9
Irregular	145.7	154.7	165.0	172.4	181.7	6.1	6.9	7.4	8.0	8.6
Regular route	5.0	4.8	4.7	4.6	4.3	0.4	0.4	0.4	0.3	0.3
Pickup and delivery	3.8	3.7	3.8	3.9	4.2	a	a	a	a	a
Own-account	114.3	113.1	123.6	123.5	119.4	3.7	3.8	3.9	4.0	4.2

a Fifty million ton-kilometers or less.
Source: Central Bureau voor de Statistiek, *Statistiek van het Binnenlands Goederenvervoer 1971* (The Hague: Staatsuitgeverij, 1972).

be specified in their license. Regular route carriers carry 2.3 percent of the tonnage and do 3.4 percent of the ton-kilometers performed.

Pickup and delivery service firms are licensed to operate within a local or regional area. They often operate in conjunction with regular route carriers at jointly maintained and jointly owned terminals.

To obtain any kind of professional license, the applicant or a director of his firm must pass a professional competency examination. Several road haulage associations and educational institutes offer courses designed to prepare a candidate for the examination, which is given twice a year. The examining committee is appointed by the government and consists of ex-government officials, representatives of users, a member of the Economic Ministry and, as secretary, an official from the principal road haulage association, Nationale Organisatie voor het Beroepsgoederenvervoer Wegtransport (NOB). This committee is supervised by a Supervisory Committee made up of representatives of government, labor, the trade associations, and users. The pass rate for the examination is only slightly better than 50 percent. (See Table N–3).

Table N–3
RESULTS OF COMPETENCY EXAMINATIONS FOR PROFESSIONAL TRUCKING LICENSE APPLICANTS

Examination	Passes	Failures	Total
Domestic examination			
September 1973			
Part A	173	110	283
Part B	166	84	250
Both parts	152		
September 1972			
Part A	159	152	311
Part B	173	97	270
International examination			
February 1974	185	34	219
October 1973	133	27	160
February 1973	191	55	246

Source: Interview with Mr. Den Harder of the Nationale Organisatie voor het Beroepsgoederenvervoer Wegtransport, Rijswijk, Z. H., 22 April 1974.

In addition, in order to secure a license the applicant must have at least 1,000 guilders capital for each ton of requested licensed capacity and a minimum of 10,000 guilders capital overall. Officially, an applicant must either own this amount or must have borrowed it on not less than a five-year contract, but in practice these requirements are difficult to enforce and applicants sometimes borrow the sum on very short-term contracts.[4]

Finally, the applicant must meet a needs test. This test is administered by the Transport Licensing Committee, Commissie Vervoer Vergunningen (CVV), a committee of independent experts, among them members of parliament, who are appointed by the Dutch government for five years. This committee is free to act independently of the Ministry of Transport but its decisions are subject to appeal to the Crown. As a consequence, the government can influence the policies and actions of the CVV, not only through its appointments but also through the appeal process.

The 1951 act requires the CVV to safeguard the interests of general transportation. These are defined in the act as the "fair and balanced consideration, with due allowance for the needs of the general public, of all interests concerned in the transport of goods."[5] The CVV has interpreted this to mean that it should ensure that "supply and demand are kept in equilibrium."[6] In making its judgments, the CVV uses five criteria: industrial production is compared with the volume of transport; ton-kilometers performed are compared with tons of licensed capacity; trends in effective freight charges are watched; the profitability of the industry as a whole is monitored; and the ratio of idle capacity to total capacity is regularly surveyed. Provided the indicators are satisfactory, which they have been to date, the CVV follows what it considers to be a liberal policy.[7]

This liberal policy is to permit expansions of capacity of existing irregular carriers if the carriers can show that within the preceding year

[4] Interview with Mr. Den Harder of the Nationale Organisatie voor het Beroepsgoederenvervoer Wegtransport, Rijswijk, Z. H., 22 April 1974.

[5] European Economic Community Commission, *Legal Status of Rail, Road and Inland Waterway Transport in the Member States of the European Economic Community: Situation at 1 July 1962* (Publications Services of the European Communities, Brussels 1963).

[6] Interview with E. W. P. Verbeek, director of the Stichting Nederlandse Internationale Wegvervoer Organisatie, 24 April 1974; interview with Mr. Bosman of the Commissie Vervoer Vergunningen, 24 April 1974.

[7] Interview with Bosman.

the firm earned a gross profit (no allowance for depreciation) of 25 percent on revenue and if they have the additional capacity to serve the needs of their shippers. The CVV acts liberally in allowing an expansion in capacity if the firm meets the profitability test. Even if the expansion of capacity is desired in order to serve customers lured from other truckers, the CVV will still grant the request.[8] Protests by other carriers have no effect in this case.

New entry, however, is difficult. A new applicant cannot, of course, show that his firm was profitable last year. Therefore the CVV compares what the new firm plans to charge with the "normalized" costs of operation. The cost figures submitted by the firm are "normalized" to include all relevant items (such as, for example, a salary for the entrepreneur). The new firm must have signed contracts with its would-be customers. Since a shipper is unlikely to sign a contract with an inexperienced firm, especially without being offered attractive rates, it is difficult for a new firm to enter the industry. If the entrepreneur does offer attractive rates, the CVV is likely to conclude that the firm will be unprofitable and is therefore likely to deny the application.

When a firm succeeds in operating for a couple of years without a license, the experience of profitable unlicensed operation can be used to justify the granting of a license. However, if the police catch the entrepreneur he is subject to fine—but it should be noted there is no cooperation between the CVV and the police.[9]

The CVV has estimated that about fifty new licenses were granted in 1972.[10] In the decade after the law was implemented, the CVV was more liberal than they have been recently, with the result that the number of firms increased about 10 percent in that period. But since 1966, as Table N–4 shows, there has been no overall increase in the number of firms, although there has been an increase in the number of international carriers.

Some irregular carriage is subject to much less stringent regulation. The regional movements of milk and vegetables from farmers to auctions and of meat from slaughterhouses to butchers are permitted under licenses granted without consideration of competency, financial stability,

---

8 Ibid.
9 Ibid.
10 Ibid.

Table N-4
NUMBER AND CAPACITY OF PROFESSIONAL TRUCKING FIRMS, 1966–72

Year (as of January)	All Firms		International License Holders	
	Number	Licensed capacity (thousands of tons)	Number	Licensed capacity (thousands of tons)
1966	11,852	394.8	1,057	69.5
1967	12,011	427.0	1,107	75.4
1968	12,086	455.9	1,157	82.1
1969	11,993	482.6	1,165	84.6
1970	11,925	513.7	1,157	90.9
1971	11,730	558.7	1,155	96.8
1972	11,405	596.1	1,197	109.3

Source: Nationale Organisatie voor het Beroepsgoederenvervoer Wegtransport, *Wegvervoer in Cijfers 1973/74* (Rijswijk, Z. H., 1973).

or profit position. It is alleged that prices and profits are low in this area.[11]

Regular route carriers are stringently controlled by the CVV. New entry is virtually impossible except on routes which are unserved. In fact, only the smallest towns do not have regular service today. An expansion of capacity is freely permitted where only one regular route carrier is serving a market, but where two or more carriers are operating, capacity expansion is strictly controlled to keep competition to a minimum. Objections by existing carriers are given great weight when the CVV considers applications to increase capacity or to extend service.[12]

Pickup and delivery services are also strictly controlled. Again, entry is virtually barred in communities being served by existing carriers. Capacity expansion is limited in order to ensure that "excessive" competition does not develop.[13]

---

[11] Ibid.
[12] Ibid.
[13] Ibid.

An additional license is required for international operations outside of the Benelux area. This license is issued by the Netherlands International Road Transport Organization (Stichting Nederlandse Internationale Wegvervoer Organisatie, NIWO). NIWO is supported by carrier fees and consists of representatives of road haulage associations, trade unions, and two representatives of the Ministry of Transport. Its decisions may be appealed to the Crown.

In order to secure an international license, an applicant must pass a special examination on international transport in addition to the exam on domestic transport. The applicant must also have sufficient capital (enough to satisfy the domestic requirement) and meet a needs test (show that shippers want the firm to haul their goods). Moreover the applicant must show that the prices its customers will be charged are high enough for a profit to be made. Costs are normalized to include a salary for the entrepreneur. According to NIWO officials, NIWO operates under the principle that shippers should have a right to choose their carrier. Thus, even if the new firm's intended customers are already customers of existing firms, the license will be given if the business is profitable. No weight is given to objections by existing carriers.[14] Nevertheless, the profit test helps protect established carriers from the competition of new firms.

Similarly, approval of requests by existing firms for an expansion in authorized capacity depends on proof of past profitability and a showing that the needs of new or old customers require the expansion. If these two criteria are met, NIWO will authorize an expansion in capacity.[15]

For international operations outside of the Benelux area, it is of course also necessary to have either a bilateral permit or European community permit. A community permit is valid for a year and permits a truck to carry goods from any country in the EEC to any other, whereas a bilateral permit is good for a trip or trips from one specific country to another specific country. West German and EEC permits are in short supply. In 1974, the Netherlands had about 627,000 trip licenses to West Germany and about 300 EEC licenses. For a carrier to receive an EEC license, it must show NIWO that it can use the license efficiently and it must exchange some of its bilateral permits for the community license.

---

[14] Interview with Verbeek.
[15] Ibid.

Only maximum rates are controlled in the Netherlands and these rates are estimated to be 50 percent above costs.[16] In international traffic, margin tariffs exist for the original six countries of the EEC but are not generally enforced.

Effects of Regulation

Unlike regulation in the other countries discussed, regulation in the Netherlands was not instituted mainly to protect the railroads. At the time before World War II when regulation was first seriously considered, railroads had already lost a substantial share of their market to road haulage. The aim of the regulation was simply to stabilize the market and prevent a recurrence of the conditions of the 1930s.

In 1971 the state railroad carried 2.2 percent of freight traffic in Holland, trucks hauled 74 percent of the traffic, and the rest went to inland water carriers (Table N–2). Even with this small share of market, the railroad has been continuing to lose market to road haulage. Its 1971 market share was down 1.5 percentage points from 1967, while motor carriers picked up 2.2 percentage points in market share in the same period. Table N–5 also indicates that professional road haulage is gaining market share at the expense of railroads.

The pattern of regulation shows the difference between the Netherlands and other countries. In West Germany, where the purpose of trucking regulation is to protect the railroads, short-distance traffic has been virtually free of capacity control, and little effort has been expended on the regulation of short-distance rates. Long-distance trucking, on the other hand, has been subject to rigorous capacity and rate controls. In the Netherlands, long-distance tramp carriage with truck-load or half truck-load lots, which is most competitive with the railroads, has been regulated the least and remains the most competitive. Capacity controls are weak for this segment of the industry, but pickup and delivery service, which is entirely local and which is complementary to, rather than competitive with, the railroads, is strictly regulated through capacity limitations wherever there are competing firms. The purpose of this regulation is to prevent "excessive" competition.

The difference between the policy on irregular transport and the policy on regular transport can be seen in the rates. Rates are freely

16 Interview with Spoel.

Table N–5

SHARE OF MODE OF TRANSPORT IN INTERNAL FREIGHT TRAFFIC FOR HIRE AND REWARD
(10 kms or more)

	1968	1969	1970	1971	1968	1969	1970	1971
	------- Millions of Metric Tons -------				------- Billions of Ton-Kilometers -------			
Road haulage	104.9	109.9	118.2	124.5	7.0	7.5	8.1	8.6
Water transport	42.6	42.2	45.9	48.0	4.3	4.5	5.0	5.0
Railroad	12.7	12.0	11.5	9.2	1.8	1.7	1.7	1.5
	------- Percentage of Total -------				------- Percentage of Total -------			
Road haulage	65	67	67	69	53	55	55	57
Water transport	27	26	26	26	33	32	34	33
Railroad	8	7	7	5	14	13	11	10

Source: Centraal Bureau voor de Statistiek, *Statistiek van het Binnenlands Goederenvervoer 1971* (The Hague: Staatsuitgeverij, 1972).

Table N–6
TYPICAL MAXIMUM TARIFFS
(Dutch guilders)

Distance		Irregular Routes		Regular Routes		
Kms	Miles	10 tons	20 tons	10 kg	50 kg	200 kg
50	31	153.95	225.70	1.91	3.08	7.25
81	50	211.05	296.55	2.06	3.35	7.95
100	62	224.70	313.55	2.06	3.35	7.95
161	100	317.60	430.85	2.33	3.83	9.19
300	186	475.85	632.25	2.76	4.63	11.27

Source: "Dokumentatie Expeditie en Transport, Uitsluitend voor EVO Leden," nos. 133-134 (The Hague: Algemene Verlaglers-en Eigen Vervoerders Organisatie, October 1970).

negotiated in both cases, but for irregular transport they tend to be about 25 to 30 percent below the official maximum (see Table N–6 for typical maximum rates).[17] Rates on regular transport, which in theory are also freely negotiated (especially for small shipments) tend to be at or near the maximum.[18] Industry spokesmen claim that the government has been slow to permit rate increases in regular transport.[19] It should be stressed that not only is capacity carefully controlled in the regular route markets but also that in most such markets there are only a few firms operating. In addition there are pairs of markets where no single firm has authority. For example, no firms have the authority to operate between Groningen in the northeast and Venlo or Maastricht in the southeast. Shipments between these points must go by more than one carrier, even though the distance is less than 200 miles.

Even though the rates appear to be high in regular route transport, profits are not. Table N–7 shows that profits as a percentage of revenue have been higher for irregular transport than for regular transport for two out of three periods. Table N–8 indicates that in recent years and for the largest size categories, profits are highest for international trans-

---

[17] Ibid.

[18] Interview with Mr. Josephus Jitta of the Algemene Verladers en Eigen Vervoerders Organisatie, The Hague, 23 April 1974.

[19] Interview with J. R. Gerritsen, public relations officer for Van Gend and Loos, 26 April 1974.

Table N–7

NET PROFIT AS A PERCENTAGE OF REVENUE FOR REGULAR, IRREGULAR, AND INTERNATIONAL TRANSPORT FIRMS, SELECTED PERIODS

Period	Regular Transport	Irregular Transport	International Transport
1960–62	4.6	6.0	n.a.
1963–65	5.2	3.3	4.5
1966–68	0.6	1.8	1.8

Source: Economisch Bureau voor het Weg- en Watervervoer, "Samenvatting Belangrijkste Onderzoekresultaten: Structuuronderzoek Beroepsgoederenvervoer de Weg," mimeographed (Rijswijk, Z. H.: Ministry of Economic Affairs, November 1973).

Table N–8

NET PROFIT AS PERCENTAGE OF REVENUE FOR REGULAR, IRREGULAR, AND INTERNATIONAL TRANSPORT, BY SIZE OF FIRM, 1970 AND 1971

Capacity of Firm (tons)	Regular Transport		Irregular Transport		International Transport	
	1970	1971	1970	1971	1971	1972
Up to 20	0.4	1.3				
20 to 60	4.7	7.2				
60 and over	4.0	3.2				
Up to 60			6.6	6.8		
60 to 120			2.0	4.2		
120 to 200			5.9	8.3		
200 and over			4.4	5.5		
Up to 100					7.0	7.4
100 to 300					4.5	5.9
300 and over					6.9	8.8

Source: Economisch Bureau voor het Weg- en Watervervoer (Rijswijk, Z. H.), "Bedrijfsuitkomsten voor het Binnenlands Geregeld en Ongeregeld Vervoer over 1970 en 1917" (January 1974) and "Rentabiliteit Grensoverschrijdend Beroepsgoederenvervoer over de Weg" (March 1974).

Table N–9

NUMBER OF BANKRUPTCIES IN ROAD HAULAGE AND FOOD RETAILING, 1968–72

Year	Road Haulage Firms	Food Retailing Firms
1968	47	97
1969	35	104
1970	40	121
1971	49	109
1972	36	146

Source: Interview with Mr. Bongers of the Centraal Bureau voor de Statistiek, Voorburg, 23 April 1974.

port, next highest for irregular transport, and lowest for regular route transport. There appears to be no simple relationship between size and profitability.

To the extent that regular route transport has lower profits than irregular route transport, the situation may be attributable to inefficiencies built into the system—inefficiencies derived from the fact that firms cannot pick up goods at intermediate points or carry goods wherever their clients wish. Using two carriers to reach a point less than 200 miles away is costly, and since rates cannot be raised to reflect the additional cost, profits must be lowered.

Bankruptcies do not seem to be high in road haulage in the Netherlands. Table N–9 shows that there has been no trend toward more or fewer bankruptcies in recent years: the rate of bankruptcy has been steady at about 0.3 percent of all trucking firms.

Spokesmen for shippers made no complaints to me about service quality.[20] Shipments to any part of Holland could easily be arranged. In the parcels area, the firm of Van Gend and Loos offers a twenty-four-hour service to anywhere in the Netherlands and claims that 94.6 percent of all its transport is carried out within that time, and 98 percent within forty-eight hours. To take advantage of the twenty-four-hour service, which is sold at the maximum rate to most customers, goods must be offered by 3:00 p.m. Also, for some 200 destinations, Van

[20] Interview with Jitta and the European shipping manager of a large American firm operating throughout Europe.

Gend and Loos offers a night express service. Goods received by Van Gend and Loos by 7:00 p.m., or in the largest towns by 9:00 to 10:30 p.m., will be delivered at the station of the town of destination by 7:00 a.m. the next morning. For this service, the company charges about two-and-a-half times the price of its normal service. About fifty tons a day go by this rate.

The Dutch have a deserved international reputation for being the leading trucking nation in western Europe. As Tables N–10 and N–11 indicate, Dutch trucks carry nearly three-quarters of the traffic crossing the borders of the Netherlands. They have about 77 percent of the professional traffic to West Germany and nearly 78 percent of the return loads. Truckers in the Netherlands have been increasing their share of the international market steadily (see Table N–10).

The preeminence of Dutch trucking suggests that the Dutch truckers offer good service. It has been alleged that it also reflects their disregard of European Economic Community rules on drivers' hours

Table N–10

COMPARISON OF DUTCH AND FOREIGN TRUCKS IN INTERNATIONAL HAULAGE ACROSS THE DUTCH BORDER, 1956–72

(millions of tons)

| Year | Dutch Trucks | | Foreign Trucks | | Dutch Percentage of Total | |
	Profes-sional	Own-account	Profes-sional	Own-account	Profes-sional	Own-account
1956	1.7	1.3	1.8	0.8	48.2	62.7
1965	9.3	3.1	5.5	2.0	62.8	60.9
1966	10.3	3.2	6.0	2.1	63.2	60.1
1967	12.3	3.4	6.5	2.2	65.3	61.3
1968	14.5	3.9	7.7	2.3	65.4	62.4
1969	16.5	4.4	6.3	2.2	72.4	67.2
1970	19.0	4.9	7.2	2.0	72.4	70.7
1971	15.0	2.7	5.7	1.0	72.4	73.2
1972	18.0	3.0	6.3	1.2	73.9	74.6

Source: Directoraat-Generaal van het Verkeer en Waterstaat, Bureau Statistiek, *Statistisch Vademecum*, no. 7 (The Hague, September 1973).

Table N–11
DUTCH SHARE OF PARTICULAR INTERNATIONAL ROAD HAULAGE MARKETS, 1972
(thousands of metric tons)

	Professional			Own-Account		
	Total	Dutch trucks	Percent-age Dutch	Total	Dutch trucks	Percent-age Dutch
Netherlands to:						
West Germany	8,836	6,808	77.0	1,836	1,366	74.4
Belgium-Luxem-bourg (1970)	3,270	2,427	74.2	889	542	61.0
France	2,092	1,443	69.0	194	167	86.1
Italy	514	326	63.4	32	25	78.1
Netherlands from:						
West Germany	8,826	6,857	77.7	1,874	1,232	65.7
Belgium-Luxem-bourg (1970)	4,345	3,121	71.8	2,219	1,693	76.3
France	1,273	796	62.5	150	124	82.7
Italy	297	200	67.3	3	2	66.7

Source: Directoraat-Generaal van het Verkeer en Waterstaat, Bureau Statistiek, *Statistisch Vademecum*, no. 7 (The Hague, September 1973).

and their relatively low tax rates.[21] No doubt these factors play a role, but the quality of their service must be good or they would not receive the business.

Within the Netherlands, professional trucking has an unusually large share of all traffic. In 1971 professional carriers handled 61.4 percent of the tons hauled and 67.9 percent of the ton-kilometers performed. Over the last five years, professional haulers have increased their share of the market both in tons and ton-kilometers (Table N–2). Yet an examination of Table N–12 indicates that own-account trucking is operated on a highly efficient basis. For trips of the same distance, the percentage of kilometers loaded seems to be uniformly higher for own-account trucking than for professional. Own-account trucking is

[21] Interview with Helmut Frech of Spedition Frech, 5 December 1973; interview with M. Dirckx, director of commercial service for Transport Coulier, Brussels, 28 January 1974.

Table N-12

ROAD HAULAGE DISTANCES IN DOMESTIC TRANSPORT, 1971

Distance (kilometers)	Professional					Own-Account				
	Thousands of tons carried	Millions of laden ton-km	Millions of km driven	Millions of km driven with load	Percentage of km loaded	Thousands of tons carried	Millions of laden ton-km	Millions of km driven	Millions of km driven with load	Percentage of km loaded
0–9	65,744	300	72.4	37.1	51	43,015	182	74.9	41.3	55
10–24	41,572	606	145.5	80.0	55	27,348	386	187.9	121.7	65
25–49	25,784	852	178.5	110.2	62	18,393	555	253.9	185.6	73
50–74	14,137	834	147.1	93.9	64	9,627	790	212.3	167.0	79
75–99	10,385	863	129.0	82.1	64	5,861	430	168.0	131.7	78
100–149	14,313	1,703	228.0	148.4	65	7,130	720	265.7	219.0	82
150–199	8,744	1,460	179.4	121.0	67	3,611	511	177.0	151.7	86
200–249	5,331	1,138	128.7	95.0	74	2,060	358	126.8	110.2	87
250–299	2,293	589	65.2	53.6	82	1,106	223	70.3	64.9	92
300 and over	1,937	588	82.4	76.5	93	1,276	306	112.5	108.8	97
Median km (50 km and over)				114.0					99.3	
Mean km loaded (50 km and over)				125.6					99.0	

Source: Centraal Bureau voor de Statistiek, *Statistiek van het Binnenlands Goederenvervoer 1971* (The Hague: Staatsuitgeverij, 1972), pp. 83–84.

apparently used only in cases where it can be used with high efficiency, which would suggest that shippers find the service received from professional transporters to be of high quality.

The largest firms in the Netherlands have grown the most rapidly, according to industry spokesmen.[22] Table N–13, which shows that the largest size category (firms operating fifteen vehicles or more) has grown most rapidly, supports this claim. The largest private firms have about 200 to 300 vehicles. However, as Table N–14 shows, they are small compared to the nationalized carrier, Van Gend and Loos, which had 1,437 and 1,375 vehicles at the end of 1971 and 1972, respectively. In 1971 Van Gend and Loos owned 2.9 percent of all vehicles owned by professional Dutch haulers. Table N–15 gives details on the distribution by size of firms. The six largest private firms (0.05 percent of all firms) owned a total of 820 vehicles (1.7 percent of all vehicles) and thus averaged about 137 vehicles per firm. Van Gend and Loos might be even larger had its growth not been artificially restrained. From 1954 to 1963 it was prohibited from increasing its capacity, and since 1963 it has only been allowed to grow with the growth in average tonnage of the industry.

Judging from the data in Table N–13, there are economies of scale up to the five-to-nine-vehicle firm size. That size category and all larger categories are growing more rapidly than the number of firms, the number of vehicles, and carrying capacity, while smaller size classes are shrinking. The largest size category has 4 percent of all firms, 31 percent of all vehicles, and 36 percent of total capacity.

These statistics understate the degree of concentration. It· has already been pointed out that the level of concentration is quite high in regular route transport, which includes some regional monopolies. Some of the regular route carriers work exclusively for larger trucking firms such as Van Gend and Loos. This company claims to have a monopoly on garment transport and is the main firm hauling new bicycles.[23]

In the irregular market there are twelve to fifteen cooperatives with a total membership of 700 to 1,000 individual firms.[24] These cooperatives allocate traffic and reduce competition among their members. A spokesman for the largest road haulage association estimated that some

---

[22] Interview with Den Harder.
[23] Interview with Gerritsen.
[24] Interview with Den Harder.

Table N-13

SIZE DISTRIBUTION OF SELECTED TRUCKING FIRMS, SELECTED YEARS

Size of Firm (number of vehicles)	Percentage of Firms			Percentage of Trucks and Tractors			Percentage of Carrying Capacity		
	1961	1968	1971	1961	1968	1971	1961	1968	1971
One	46	41	39	16	11	9	13	8	6
Two	21	18	16	14	9	8	13	8	6
Three or Four	19	20	19	22	18	15	22	16	14
Five to Nine	10	15	17	22	24	25	24	26	25
Ten to Fourteen	2	3	5	9	11	12	11	12	13
Fifteen	2	3	4	17	27	31	17	30	36

Note: The aggregate data on firms, vehicles, and capacity are as follows:

Year	Number of Firms	Number of Trucks and Tractors	Carrying Capacity (tons)
1961	11,167	32,932	266,982
1968	11,993	45,243	482,588
1971	11,405	48,788	596,046

Source: Economisch Bureau voor het Weg- en Watervervoer, "Samenvatting Belangrijkste Onderzoekresultaten: Structuuronderzoek Beroepsgoederenvervoer de Weg," mimeographed (Rijswijk, Z. H.: Ministry of Economic Affairs, November 1973), p. 67.

Table N–14

SELECTED STATISTICS ON NATIONALIZED TRUCKING FIRM OF VAN GEND AND LOOS, 1969–72

Item	1969	1970	1971	1972
Number of employees	5,292	5,423	5,228	4,995
Number of vehicles	1,569	1,485	1,437	1,375
Number of trailers and semi-trailers	285	306	287	335
Total revenues (1,000 DG)	145,000	174,000	192,000	204,000
Profits				
After taxes (1,000 DG)	2,712	3,152	4,705	5,167
As a percentage of revenues	1.9	1.8	2.5	2.5
As a percentage of capital and reserves for year	7.3	7.5	9.8	9.4

Note: Totals as of 31 December of each year.
Source: N–14: Van Gend and Loos, *Annual Report 1972*.

70 to 80 percent of the firms with only one or two vehicles worked exclusively for another firm, either a shipper or another trucking firm.[25] Most of the rest are in local transport, especially in construction and in the dump truck business.

It is known that holding companies control many large trucking firms both in Holland and abroad. Reportedly English firms are purchasing Dutch trucking enterprises [26] and large Dutch firms also own enterprises abroad. Van Gend and Loos has a subsidiary in New York (100 percent owned), three subsidiaries in Belgium (90, 50, and 35 percent owned), and one each in Denmark (49 percent owned), England (47 percent owned), and France (40 percent owned).[27]

Although concentration is much higher than it would appear to be from the statistics, it is not so high as to prevent active competition within the field of irregular transport. However, there is evidence of some monopoly in the regular route market brought about by regulation.

---

25 Ibid.

26 Interview with Spoel.

27 Van Gend and Loos, *Annual Report 1972*.

Table N–15

SIZE DISTRIBUTION OF PROFESSIONAL TRUCKING FIRMS, 1971

Vehicles per Firm	Number of Firms	Number of Vehicles	Capacity of Firms (tons)
One	4,455	4,455	38,146
Two	1,847	3,694	37,661
Three	1,315	3,945	42,609
Four	899	3,596	38,930
Five	680	3,400	39,743
Six	453	2,718	31,747
Seven	313	2,191	28,455
Eight	260	2,080	25,172
Nine	174	1,566	20,315
Ten	165	1,650	21,837
Eleven	125	1,375	18,153
Twelve	100	1,200	16,336
Thirteen	58	754	9,926
Fourteen	63	882	11,025
Fifteen to nineteen	181	3,015	42,647
Twenty to forty-nine	270	7,554	116,505
Fifty to ninety-nine	40	2,450	38,444
100 or more	7	2,263	18,395
Total	11,405	48,788	596,046

Source: Centraal Bureau voor de Statistiek, *Statistiek van het Binnenlands Goederenvervoer 1971* (The Hague: Staatsuitgeverij, 1972), p. 79.

Conclusion

Regulation has not protected the railroads from trucking competition and was not intended for this purpose. Rather it was intended to stabilize the industry, and the industry is stable. Whether regulation was necessary to stabilize the industry cannot be proven from the available data. In the regular route market one objective of regulation was to foster a network of trucking routes to handle the parcels trade. The idea was to have the more profitable routes cross-subsidize the more unprofitable. It is claimed that regulation has produced this result,[28] and the overall mediocre rate of profit earned by this segment of the industry does suggest that cross-subsidization may be taking place. In the absence of a rate ceiling, however, such cross-subsidization would not be necessary.

The restrictions on competition within the pickup and delivery area seem less comprehensible. Even in areas having only one licensed pickup and delivery firm, the possibility of own-account trucking, especially in a short-haul market, reduces the monopoly power of any single firm. There are no known data on the profits of, or the rates charged by, pickup and delivery firms.

The Dutch claim that one of the most noteworthy aspects of their system is the emphasis on examinations of professional competency.[29] They claim that this emphasis produces skilled entrepreneurs and explains in part the excellent performance of Dutch truckers in international haulage. In fact, in the Netherlands, passing a professional competency exam is required in most fields, including retailing. It does seem likely that competency requirements lead to a trucking industry of better quality than would exist otherwise, but whether the requirements are desirable is another question, since it is doubtful that government regulation should impose a higher quality standard than that for which shippers would willingly pay.

---

[28] Interview with van der Noordt.
[29] Interview with Jitta; interview with H. J. Noortman, director of the Stichting Nederlands Vervoerwetenschappelijk Institut, 1 April 1974.

5

Regulation in Sweden

Regulation in Sweden has followed a pattern similar to that of regulation in other countries. By the late 1930s the railroads were suffering from considerable competition from road haulage. In 1940, mainly to protect the railroads, but also to restrict competition within the road haulage industry, parliament enacted a law regulating the professional trucking industry. That law is still on the books, but amendments and government rulings have led to considerable changes in the interpretation and effects of the law.

The law of 1940 established one central licensing authority, along with regional licensing authorities for each of Sweden's twenty-four counties. A firm licensed in a particular county was and is authorized to carry goods anywhere within that county and to and from that county, but it is not allowed to load goods in another county for delivery anywhere but to its home county.

Originally, an applicant could enter the industry if he was fit and if there was a need for his services. Every application to start a trucking business or to expand capacity was published and sent to both the local trucking association and the state railroad for their views on the need for the proposed service. In making its decision, the licensing authority acted in part on the view that if vehicles were used less than 170 hours per month, there was no clear need for further authorized capacity.[1]

As a result it was very difficult for a new firm to secure a license. Even efficient firms already in existence had difficulty in expanding their authorized capacity. During the 1950s the licensing authorities

[1] Interview with Lars Kritz of the Industriens Utredningsinstitut, 12 March 1974.

often restricted the licensed vehicle to carrying certain goods, a restriction which reduced efficiency and contributed to a desire to liberalize the system.

Even though professional trucking capacity was strictly controlled, the railroads failed to benefit measurably. By the 1950s the state railroad began to lose money and the railroad freight business stagnated. In 1950 the railroads carried 38.2 million tons; over the next nine years this increased only to 38.4 million tons—although subsequently business did pick up.[2]

In 1953 the government appointed a commission to review transport policy. The commission submitted its first report in 1961, eight years later, and its second report in 1962. A majority of the commission's members wanted a more liberal policy than the one in effect. They found that the existing system of regulation had succeeded in fostering regional monopolies and in frustrating the desires of existing operators to expand. Reportedly some licenses sold for 15,000 to 25,000 Swedish kronor (about $3,000 to $5,000).[3]

At that time, even the road haulage association favored liberalization so that its most efficient members could expand. Railroad opposition to liberalization was mollified when the railroads were offered considerable independence. The rail network was to be divided into a commercial section, which was intended to cover its costs, and a noncommercial section, which was to be supported through government grants. On the commercial network, the state railroad was to be given freedom to negotiate rates with individual shippers without publication, and its common carrier obligation was removed.[4]

In 1963 parliament enacted the commission's recommendations and established three phases for decontrol. For the first two years, the licensing authorities were to increase capacity by 15 percent per year. During 1966 and 1967, capacity was to be increased by 20 percent per year. In the third phase, starting in 1968, the needs test was to be removed and there was to be a tax system that levied the social costs, including environmental, on each mode of transport.

For a variety of reasons the third phase was never implemented, although in 1968 the licensing authorities were told to operate within

---

[2] Sweden, Official Statistics, State Railways Board, *The Railways of Sweden 1971* (Stockholm, 1972), p. 31.

[3] Interview with Kritz.

[4] Ibid.

the spirit of the 1963 act.[5] In practice this meant that from 1965 to 1973 the licensing authorities were liberal and entry into the trucking industry was virtually free.

The major reason the third phase was never put into effect was a fear that excess capacity was developing and that too many inexperienced small operators were going in and out of the business.[6] Apparently there was a sharp rise in the number of new, one-vehicle firms. From 1965 to 1968 the number of one-truck firms increased by 25 percent while the number of firms with two to five trucks increased 13 percent. The total number of firms increased 21 percent, or 6.5 percent annually, over this period. This increase in the number of firms was reportedly coupled with a decline in industry profits, a rise in bankruptcies, and a decline in freight rates.[7]

Officially the postponement of the third stage was the result of a failure to determine the appropriate costs to be levied on the trucking industry. Nevertheless, there was concern with the state of the industry, though a 1971 government study concluded that the way to deal with low profits by small firms was not to increase regulation but to restrict credit, encourage cooperatives, and to extend employment benefits to small truckers.[8] Low profitability was considered to be a transitional phenomenon which would disappear as the industry rationalized its structure.

Critics of the 1963 act have claimed that the flock of new entrants resulted in excess capacity. Lars Kritz in an article published in *Vär Industri* carefully analyzed this assertion.[9] He found that while professional capacity did increase rapidly during the 1960s, own-account capacity did not, and the net increase in capacity was in line with historical trends. Specifically he found that total carrying capacity increased at an annual rate of 5.0 percent from 1955 to 1959, 7.3 percent from 1960 to 1964, and 4.7 percent annually from 1965 to 1971. In other words, total capacity increased at a slower rate after liberalization than before. According to Kritz, one major effect of liberalization was to shift traffic from own-account vehicles to professional truckers.

---

[5] Ibid.

[6] Ibid.

[7] Sweden, Department of Transportation, *Lastbil och Taxi* (Statens Offentliga Utredningar 1971:34).

[8] Ibid.

[9] Lars Kritz, "Transportpolitikon," *Vär Industri*, no. 10 (1972).

Table S–1
SWEDISH FREIGHT TRAFFIC, BY MODE, 1966–72

	Millions of Tons				Billions of Ton-Kilometers			
Year	Rail-roads	Profes-sional	Own-account	Total	Rail-roads	Profes-sional	Own-account	Total
1966	59	n.a.	n.a.	—	14.1	11.2	4.3	15.5
1967	59	n.a.	n.a.	—	13.5	12.2	n.a.	—
1968	65	n.a.	n.a.	—	14.8	14.0	n.a.	—
1969	68	n.a.	n.a.	—	16.0	15.0	n.a.	—
1970	71	297[a]	170[a]	467[a]	17.3	11.8[a]	4.9[a]	16.7[a]
1971	64	—	—	—	15.7	—	—	—
1972	n.a.	304	150	453	n.a.	14.0	4.2	18.2

[a] New Series figures, which are statistically much superior to earlier figures. For 1970, only second half is estimated. Year total is double. Includes estimates for vans with less than two-ton capacity.

Source: National Central Bureau of Statistics, *Statistical Reports,* SM/T 1973:32 and NrT 1973:33.

According to his statistics professional carriers had about 45 percent of the carrying capacity in 1960, 47 percent by 1965, and 56 percent by 1971. Table S–1 shows that in 1970 professional haulers were carrying 64 percent of tonnage and 71 percent of ton-kilometers. By 1972 they were carrying 67 percent of tonnage and 77 percent of ton-miles, while professional capacity was 55 percent of the total.

Several observers have pointed out that not all of the increase in number of new firms during the 1960s came from new entrants.[10] A number of illegal, unlicensed firms took advantage of the liberalization to become licensed. Even so, many of the new license holders were in fact new firms. The statistics indicate that after a rush of new firms to enter the industry between 1965 and 1968, the rate of entry slowed down. As Table S–2 shows, the net annual increase in the number of firms dropped from a peak in 1967 of 1,369 to 697 in 1968 to 170 in 1969. Since then the net annual increase in the number of firms has fluctuated between 367 and 194.

One problem in the interpretation of the 1963 liberalization is to separate its effects from the effects of changes in business activity.

[10] Ibid.

Table S–2
ENTRY AND EXIT OF TRUCKING FIRMS, 1953–72

| Year | Net Increase in Number of Firms | Bankruptcies | |
		Number	Percent of firms
1953–63 annual average	342	n.a.	n.a.
1964	1,013	n.a.	n.a.
1965	1,068	n.a.	n.a.
1966	697	n.a.	n.a.
1967	1,369	n.a.	n.a.
1968	697	66	0.37
1969	170	88	0.47
1970	367	96	0.51
1971	343	123	0.64
1972	194	194	0.99

Source: Data from Svenska Akeriförbundet, *Stockholmskongressen 1973* (Stockholm, 1973), p. 11; and Lars Kritz, "Transportpolitikon," *Vär Industri,* no. 10 (1972), p. 23.

Gross domestic product in Sweden was increasing at a rapid rate in the first half of the 1960s, reaching a peak rate of growth in 1964. During the next two years, which coincided with the start of liberalization, growth slowed considerably, so that the decline in the profits of the trucking industry could just as well be the result of a business slowdown as of a large increase in capacity.

The number of trucking bankruptcies and their proportion to the total number of trucking firms has increased steadily since 1968 (see Table S–2). In 1969, the Swedish economy turned down sharply. The growth in business activity ceased by 1971 and unemployment rates reached substantial levels by the first quarter of 1972. The record number of bankruptcies for 1972 would appear to be tied in with the poor performance of the Swedish economy.

Partly because of the reputedly poor economic situation of the professional trucking industry and representations to that effect from the road haulage association, and partly because of pressure from organized labor, the government tightened entry requirements on 1 October 1972.[11] Labor was concerned with the large number of non-

11 Interview with Kritz; interview with Gunnar Himmelstrand of the Näringslivets Trafikdelegation, 19 March 1974.

union owner-drivers and hoped that tighter regulation would foster larger enterprises fewer in number that would be subject to unionization.[12]

Since 1 October 1972, when new regulations became effective, some of the licensing authorities have become more restrictive.[13] The applicant must be a fit person, have experience, and have sufficient economic and financial resources. While the law only requires an applicant to describe his "kind of activity," in order to be permitted to expand authorized capacity or to enter the industry, in practice, the applicant must show that specific shippers wish to use his services.[14] These shippers, however, can be currently served by other carriers. A semi-public organization (jointly financed by business and the government) must have approved a financial plan showing that the applicant's operation will cover its costs. A licensing authority can deny a license whenever there is excess capacity, but the decision of the authority is subject to appeal. In recent years there have been at least 300 appeals per year, with an increase in the number in 1972 and 1973.[15] Reputedly some licensing authorities have tightened entry requirements considerably, while others still claim to be very liberal.[16]

No doubt part of the increased number of appeals from licensing decisions are the result of the more rigid requirements for securing a license or for obtaining permission to increase capacity. Part, however, are the result of a rush of new applicants produced when many unlicensed carriers attempted to secure licenses. In 1972 shippers were made subject to fine if they used unlicensed carriers, and as a consequence, it is likely that many gypsy firms have been seeking licenses.[17]

The government enforced a maximum tariff until October 1972, but since that time has required only that the Swedish road haulage association announce increases in its recommended tariffs. It is claimed that the maximum tariffs were meaningless, since proposed rises in this tariff were automatically approved.[18]

---

[12] Interview with Himmelstrand.

[13] Interview with Kritz.

[14] Interview with Mr. Palmgren, Stockholm County Licensing Authority, March 1974.

[15] Interview with Jan Johnsson of the Department of Transportation, Stockholm, March 1974.

[16] Ibid.

[17] Ibid.

[18] Ibid.

As was pointed out above, licensed trucks are authorized to carry goods anywhere within their home counties and to and from their home counties but not between other parts of Sweden. In 1972, 86 percent of the tonnage carried by professional haulers moved within the haulers' home counties. Much of the freight moving between counties is handled by freight forwarding companies offering regularly scheduled service. This service requires a license if it is offered more than twice a week between any two points. Such a license specifies the number of trips that can be made per week but does not limit the number of trucks that can be used on any trip.

To secure a regular-route freight-forwarding license is difficult. An applicant must have large financial resources, must show a need for the service, and must show that he is capable of performing it.[19] If good service is already operating on the proposed route, an application is likely to be denied.[20]

There are two large firms, A. B. Godstrafik och Bilspedition and A. B. Svenska Godscentraler (ASG) which together carry about 90 percent of the long-distance parcels traffic. Recently a new firm succeeded in receiving licenses and has begun to challenge the established firms. Operating out of the Stockholm area there are less than fifteen firms authorized to offer regular-route freight-forwarding service to other specific points. Depending on the county of destination, these freight forwarders carry between 18 and 66 percent of the tons going from the Stockholm area; on average they handle 28 percent of all such traffic.[21] Freight forwarders account for just under 3 percent of all tonnage carried by professional truckers.

The Effect of the System

Published studies of the effect of the 1963 liberalization have been discussed above. Trucking industry spokesmen claim that profits have been depressed for the last decade, that rates have declined, and that excess capacity has grown.[22] As Kritz has shown, capacity has not

---

[19] Interview with Palmgren.

[20] Ibid.

[21] Computed from figures in the National Central Bureau of Statistics, *Statistical Reports*, NrT 1973:33 and NT 1973:21.

[22] Interview with Jan Johannessen of the Svenska Åkeriförbundet, Stockholm, March 1974.

111

Table S–3

SELECTED STATISTICS ON SWEDISH
TRUCKING ENTERPRISES, 1971

Number of enterprises in sample	2,440
Average number of employees during year	25,092
Value added (millions of kronor)	1,539.5
Gross income (millions of kronor)	2,326.6
Reported net profit (after tax) (millions of kronor)	29.0
Profit as percentage of income	1.2
Capital and reserves (millions of kronor)	172.7
Profit as percentage of capital and reserves	16.8

Source: National Central Bureau of Statistics, *Enterprises 1971* (Stockholm, 1973).

grown faster after 1965 than it grew before. The decline in profits can be attributed to general economic decline as well as to regulatory changes. However, if regulation had fostered monopoly, as was claimed, then easier access to the market was likely to erode monopoly profits and return profits to more normal levels. A reduction in freight rates would be likely to accompany any increase in capacity or improved efficiency resulting from easier entry. Improvements in highways and in trucking technology over this period could have been expected to reduce real rates even without changes in regulation.

Table S–3 reports on the income of trucking enterprises. Net profits as a percentage of revenue appear to be low, but not when they are compared with other Swedish businesses, and profits as a return on capital are substantial; in fact, they are higher than those for any other country where figures are available. Net profits as a percentage of revenue are 0.4 for construction and retail trade, 0.3 for wholesale trade, 0.2 for restaurants and hotels, and 1.5 for all manufacturing.[23]

As Kritz pointed out, the capacity of professional trucking has grown both absolutely and as a percentage of total trucking capacity. An increase in capacity would be unlikely if profits were not sufficient to attract investment. Capacity growth is, however, sensitive to demand. In 1971 real gross domestic product declined for the first time in quite a few years; for the first time also total capacity of the trucking industry

---

[23] National Central Bureau of Statistics, *Enterprises 1971* (1973).

Table S–4

ACTUAL ROAD HAULAGE RATES IN SWEDEN, 1967–73

(Swedish kronor per 100 kilograms)

Length of Trip (miles)	Year						
	1967	1968	1969	1970	1971	1972	1973
80	2.25	2.25	2.25	2.25	2.88	2.58	2.92
180	3.74	3.74	3.74	3.74	3.76	3.98	4.16
200	3.86	3.86	3.86	3.86	3.90	4.10	4.46
300	5.04	5.04	5.04	5.04	5.52	5.79	6.06

Note: Rates given are for a 10-ton load of manufactured palletized product.
Source: Data from the files of a major shipper.

fell (by 3.0 percent).[24] As business picked up in 1972, trucking industry capacity grew by 4.9 percent. During the period from 1970 to 1972 total ton-kilometers of road haulage (professional and own-account) increased 9 percent while total industry capacity went up only 1.7 percent.

Actual freight rates paid by one shipper are shown in Table S–4 and the rates suggested by the road haulage association in Table S–5. Actual rates are about half of the suggested level. Adjusted for inflation, actual rates declined from 1967 through 1971, then rose slightly in 1972 and fell again in 1973. Presumably, with a higher price for oil, they have increased since. In real terms they were considerably lower in 1973 than in 1967, with rates for the longest distance down about 12 percent. These figures are certainly consistent with a shift from a monopolistic to a competitive industry.

Service quality is reputedly good. Shippers report no difficulty in securing good service to anywhere in Sweden including any remote areas reachable by road. ASG claims that they will deliver within twenty-four hours anywhere in Sweden except the far north and that goods shipped by 3:00 p.m. will, for 90 percent of the market, be delivered the next day.

Further evidence on the quality of service comes from data on own-account shipping. In 1970 only 36 percent of the tons and 29 percent of the ton-kilometers carried by road went by own-account truck-

---

[24] National Central Bureau of Statistics, *Statistical Reports*, NT 1973:36.

Table S–5
SOME LONG DISTANCE RATES SUGGESTED BY THE
ROAD HAULAGE ASSOCIATION
(Swedish kronor per 1000 kilograms)

Distance		Shipment Size		
Kilometers	Miles	10 tons	15 tons	20 tons
50	31	3.40	3.30	3.30
81	50	3.60	3.50	3.50
100	62	4.20	4.00	4.00
161	100	5.10	5.00	5.00
323	200	8.30	7.90	7.90
806	500	15.80	14.50	14.50

Source: Svenska Åkeriförbundet, "Normaltaxa för Fjärrtrafik," 1974–03–01.

ing. By 1972 the share of own-account trucking had fallen to 33 percent of the tons and 23 percent of the ton-kilometers. These figures indicate considerable consumer satisfaction with professional trucking.

Table S–6 shows that own-account trucks are loaded for a higher proportion of the kilometers moved than are professional trucks but with a smaller average load for each size of truck. On average, own-account trucks move on much shorter hauls than do professional trucks and drive fewer miles per year. These facts indicate that own-account trucks are used mainly where they can achieve reasonably full utilization mainly on short haul; they are undoubtedly used only when special factors make their use particularly advantageous. Rates charged by professional truckers are evidently not so high as to make own-account trucking an attractive alternative to the use of common carriers. Probably because of the 1963 liberalization, trends in market structure in Sweden have not followed the pattern found elsewhere. As can be seen from Table S–7, the proportion of firms with one license has actually increased since 1960. The proportion with two to five vehicles has, however, declined since 1965. There has been the usual growth in number of large firms and in the importance of the largest size categories. There would appear to be clear diseconomies of scale for firms with two to five vehicles.

114

Table S-6
ROAD TRANSPORT, BY CAPACITY OF VEHICLE, 1972

Carrying Capacity (tons)	Number of Vehicles	Weight Carried (millions of tons)	Average Speed (kph)	Percent of Kilometers Loaded	Mean Haulage Distance (km)	Mean Load (tons)	Percent of Utilized Capacity Taken	Average Run per Vehicle (km)	Average Hours of Vehicle Use	Average Ton-Km/Vehicle	Average Revenue/Vehicle (kronor)
					Professional Transport						
2–3.9	1,768	1.4	15.2	77	36	1.8	45	19,906	1,328	27,668	53,117
4–4.9	1,626	2.9	11.7	75	21	2.9	49	17,018	1,481	37,573	66,226
5–5.9	3,301	13.1	15.7	64	15	4.2	44	21,744	1,402	58,581	60,065
6–6.9	2,748	12.7	18.0	70	19	4.6	39	27,100	1,500	87,489	76,357
7–7.9	3,672	28.1	19.0	65	24	8.9	47	31,589	1,658	182,236	80,219
8–9.9	6,508	59.5	23.9	70	39	12.0	51	43,041	1,795	360,000	106,953
10–11.9	4,607	63.4	29.1	62	52	19.0	52	59,815	2,067	709,761	138,938
Over 12	8,283	122.5	29.6	66	58	20.6	52	63,261	2,132	860,455	152,938
Total	32,511	303.5									
Average			24.0	67	46	14.9	51	43,209	1,798	429,174	107,877
					Own-account Transport						
2–3.9	11,572	6.0	16.3	79	39	1.5	41	17,009	1,046	20,271	
4–4.9	4,383	4.4	11.6	83	33	2.8	51	14,669	1,256	33,444	
5–5.9	4,632	10.3	16.7	71	22	3.4	42	20,483	1,223	49,563	
6–6.9	4,288	12.9	16.8	76	26	4.2	46	24,817	1,461	78,448	
7–7.9	3,043	15.0	20.9	69	25	6.2	45	30,848	1,465	131,740	
8–9.9	3,264	25.6	23.1	65	29	9.4	47	37,852	1,658	228,725	
10–11.9	2,572	30.5	25.7	61	33	13.8	49	46,915	1,825	392,696	
Over 12	2,521	38.1	27.9	58	29	16.6	47	46,253	1,675	441,724	
Total	36,277	143.6									
Average			19.0	70	29	6.6	47	25,281	1,332	116,276	

Source: National Central Bureau of Statistics, *Statistical Reports*, NrT 1973:33.

115

Table S–7
SIZE DISTRIBUTION OF TRUCKING FIRMS,
VARIOUS YEARS, 1953–72

Size of Firms (number of vehicles)	Year					
	1953	1960	1965	1970	1971	1972
------------ Percentage of Firms by Size Class ------------						
One	69.0	68.0	68.2	71.6	71.6	71.5
Two to five	28.0	28.3	27.2	23.7	23.6	23.5
Six to ten	1.4	2.4	3.0	2.8	2.9	3.0
Eleven to fifteen	0.4	0.6	0.8	0.9	0.9	1.0
Sixteen and over	0.4	0.7	0.8	1.0	1.0	1.0
----------- Percentage of Vehicles by Firm Size -----------						
One	n.a.	36.7	34.3	35.2	35.1	35.0
Two to five	n.a.	38.8	36.0	31.0	30.7	30.6
Six to ten	n.a.	9.6	11.3	10.5	10.7	11.0
Eleven to fifteen	n.a.	3.8	4.8	5.4	5.5	5.8
Sixteen and over	n.a.	11.1	13.6	17.9	18.0	17.6
Number of firms	10,045	13,099	15,888	19,180	19,523	19,717
Number with more than 100 vehicles	0	0	3	4	n.a.	n.a.
Number of vehicles	n.a.	24,296	31,616	39,042	39,853	40,325

Source: Data from Svenska, Åkeriförbundet, *Stockholmskongressen 1973,* p. 10, and *Lastbil och Taxi* (Statens Offentliga Utredningar 1971:34), pp. 52–53.

The usual diseconomies of one-vehicle firms are not present in Sweden because of several particularities of the market. About 54 percent of the one-vehicle firms belong to trucking centrals (see Table S–8), generally cooperatives that operate as large single firms. The average truck central is owned by thirty-eight haulers and has fifty-seven trucks.[25] Table S–9 shows the size of truck centrals. These centrals are important, because they set prices, sign contracts, and often own subsidiary operations. As a consequence, over half the one-vehicle firms are independent firms in law, but not in fact.

In addition, both ASG and Bilspedition own almost no trucks themselves but hire independent truckers who work only for them under

[25] Svenska Åkeriförbundet, "Some Facts about Transport of Goods," mimeographed (Stockholm, n.d.).

Table S–8
MARKET STRUCTURE OF PROFESSIONAL TRANSPORT

	All Professional Firms		Members of Truck Centrals			
Size of Company (number of vehicles)	Number of companies	Number of vehicles	Number of companies	Number of vehicles	Percentage of companies	Percentage of vehicles
One	14,100	14,100	7,590	7,590	53.8	53.8
Two to five	4,625	12,327	2,357	6,256	51.0	50.8
Six to ten	595	4,482	237	1,729	39.8	38.6
Eleven to fifteen	191	2,333	52	652	27.2	27.9
16 and over	206	7,083	33	867	16.0	12.2
Total	19,717	40,325	10,269	17,094	52.1	42.4

Source: *Svenska Åkeriförbundet Informerar* (U 1973:6), p. 3.

one-year contracts. These truckers are in practice simply employees of the two large firms, although they receive a percentage of the revenue—about 85 percent. They hire a total of between 5,000 and 6,000 trucks—most of which belong to single-vehicle firms. Of the roughly 14,000 one-vehicle firms, some 12,000 either are in truck centrals or working for one of the two big freight forwarders.

ASG, which is 67.5 percent owned by the Swedish Railroad, earned a 3 percent rate of profit on its revenue of 741,162,000 Swedish kronor

Table S–9
SIZE OF TRUCK CENTRALS, 1971 AND 1972

Size of Central (number of trucks)	Number of Truck Centrals	
	1971	1972
0 to 24	62	64
25 to 49	112	105
50 to 99	81	87
100 and over	44	40
Total	299	296

Source: *Svenska Åkeriförbundet Informerar* (U 1973:6), table 4.

in 1972.[26] This is considerably above the industry average of 1.2 percent. While company policy is to own no vehicles, in 1974 ASG owned about 150 that they had taken over because of failures by their owners.[27]

In actual practice concentration in Swedish trucking is higher than would appear to be the case from the data on the number of companies. In short-distance transport (under 100 kilometers), which is about 91 percent of all trucking, transport is sold by about 600 independent entities. There are about 300 trucking centrals and about 300 large trucking companies that handle almost all the local business.[28] The largest trucking company, with 1,050 vehicles in 1970, is Svelast, a wholly owned subsidiary of the Swedish Railroad, which specializes in pickup and delivery, especially from the railroads.[29] There are only four companies in Sweden with more than 100 vehicles, but there are 40 truck centrals.

Truck centrals, their members, or their subsidiaries, own 77 percent (nearly 900) of the gravel pits. Together they own about 200 dumpers, over 600 excavators, and over 2,300 loaders. Altogether in 1972 they owned or controlled 17,632 trucks and 7,364 trailers—over half the trucks and tractors owned by professional trucking firms.[30]

In specific local markets concentration is even higher than these figures would indicate. In two counties there is only one truck central, and in each case the truck central has over 100 members.[31] There are four other counties with six or fewer truck centrals. It was claimed that in some northern counties truck centrals have more or less a monopoly.[32] On the other hand, it is generally true that there are large private companies outside the truck centrals as well as a few individual truckers outside the system.

The truck centrals do not act as monopolists. If they were attempting to monopolize the business they could be expected to encourage all trucking firms in an area to join the central. But in fact they usually will not accept new members, unless the new members bring a significant

---

[26] A. B. Svenska Godscentraler (ASG), *Annual Report 1972.*

[27] Interview with a spokesman for A. B. Svenska Godscentraler (ASG), March 1974.

[28] *Svenska Åkeriförbundet Informerar* (U 1973:6), table 4.

[29] Svenska Åkeriförbundet, "Transport of Goods in Sweden," mimeographed (Stockholm, n.d.), p. 3.

[30] *Svenska Åkeriförbundet Informerar* (U 1973:6), p. 4.

[31] Ibid., table 4.

[32] Interview with Johnsson.

number of new customers. Thus they would appear to be designed to take advantage of marketing and administrative economies of scale. As long as entry was fairly easy, no monopoly was possible. In the future, however, if regulation blocks new entry, these centrals may become the focus of attempts to monopolize local markets.

The long-distance markets are dominated by the two giants, ASG and Bilspedition. Regulation hinders new firms from entering the long-distance regular-route market, although individual trucks can ply between their home county and other localities in Sweden. These two companies handle long-distance truck-load lots as well as parcels, but in truck-load lots they do not seem to have the dominant position that they hold in the parcels business.

Even though concentration is high in the long-distance market and even though entry is virtually barred through regulation, competition still plays a role. The two dominant companies compete with each other and with some much smaller competitors, and this apparently makes the market a competitive one. On some business the discount can go as high as 50 percent from the published tariff.[33] Users of the two companies do not believe that they face a monopoly and often find they can play one of the companies off against another.[34]

For local markets, the road haulage association publishes recommended tariffs. These are widely discounted although no data exist on the extent of discounting.[35] In general published tariffs serve as maximum tariffs to be paid only by the small occasional shipper.

Conclusion

The regulatory changes of the 1960s injected considerable new competitive pressures into the Swedish trucking industry. The result has been that service and rates have improved to such an extent that professional trucking has attracted a considerable amount of freight previously carried on own-account.

Although the trucking industry still retains elements of monopoly, mainly because of regulation, competitive behavior prevails. The indus-

---

[33] Interview with Mr. Rollen of A. B. Svenska Godscentraler (ASG), March 1974.
[34] Interview with Mr. Ringbouy of Ringbouy Company, March 1974.
[35] Ibid.

try has developed some interesting institutional arrangements for combining small firms to benefit from the economies of scale in marketing, pricing, and managing trucking operations. Both the trucking central and the two large freight forwarding companies offer the advantage of individually owned and maintained vehicles with centralized administration and control. The result is a highly efficient operation and trucking system.

6

Comparisons

The chapters so far have examined the trucking regulatory system in five European countries. In each were described the unique features and the historical background of regulation and of the trucking industry in a particular country. Some lessons were drawn about the impact of regulation or changes in regulation. This chapter looks at the effect of regulation by contrasting the system and industry performance in these countries.

Regulation is, of course, only one variable affecting transportation in each country. There is a wide variety of other factors leading to differences among the trucking industries. The geographical distributions of industry, ports, and population in the various countries clearly lead to differences. The size of the country, the composition of industry output, the country's agricultural product, and its network of rail lines, waterways, and roads all have their effect.

The transport industries are specialized service institutions developed to deal with the specific needs of each country. In reality we should not speak of a "transport industry" but of a multitude of industries serving the individual needs of specific shippers. The composition of the transport industries reflects the composition of industry demand for transportation. As industry demand differs, so will the transportation industry differ.

Finally and with some reluctance I must add that there are differences derived from disparities in national attitudes about work, travel, and discipline. As an economist I would prefer to attribute variation in industry behavior to divergences in economic conditions, but personal observation and the existence of large and otherwise inexplicable differences force the conclusion that national attitudes do lead to disparities.

This chapter attempts to isolate the effects of regulation on the trucking industry and its customers. For the reasons cited above it is difficult to infer the effect of regulation from the welter of statistics. Moreover, the figures themselves are often not directly comparable, and among the figures profit and bankruptcy statistics are particularly suspect. For example, in Sweden reported profits are 1.2 percent of revenue, while in Great Britain for a sample of firms they have averaged about 11 percent. But in Sweden the return on capital after taxes was equal to 16.8 percent in 1971, while the average rate of return for eight companies in England for the same year was 17.8 percent *before taxes* and the five-year average was 14.6 percent before taxes. Differences may stem in part from differences in depreciation and in other aspects of accounting allowed under the tax systems of the two countries.

As can be seen from Table C–1, Great Britain and West Germany are about the same size, Belgium and the Netherlands have about the same population and area, while Sweden is larger in square miles than any other country of the five and smaller in population. Industry and population are more spread out in West Germany than in Great Britain, and hence freight movements are longer and total ton-miles carried are over 50 percent higher there than in Great Britain.

Each of the five regulatory systems has unique features, but probably the single best indicator of regulatory constraint is the rate of entry. Little regulation in a growing industry such as trucking will lead to a high rate of entry, while strict controls will prevent or retard entry.

Great Britain has virtually no control over entry except for minor quality qualifications designed to improve road safety. While good figures do not exist on the number of completely new firms entering the British market, it would nevertheless appear that the rate of entry is substantially higher than in other countries.

West Germany would appear to be at the other extreme. It is the only country in the study which has controls on minimum and maximum freight rates. Entry is virtually impossible except by purchase of an existing firm. Such a purchase involves payment of a large sum reflecting the value of the restrictions on entry. Clearly, regulation has produced monopoly gains that are capitalized into the value of licenses.

Belgium would appear to have almost an open market. Regulation tends to delay, but not to preclude, entry. As Table C–2 shows, the

Table C–1
SELECTED STATISTICS FOR FIVE EUROPEAN COUNTRIES, 1971

Item	Great Britain	West Germany	Bel-gium	The Nether-lands	Sweden
Population (millions)	55.7	61.3	9.7	13.2	8.1
Area (thousands of square miles)	95.9	94.3	11.8	12.9	173.4
Miles of principal roads (thousands)	29.2	23.0	6.7	2.5	7.7
Miles of expressway (thousands)	0.7	2.8	0.3	0.7	0.3
Miles of railroads (thousands)	11.8	18.2	2.6	2.0	7.1
Freight traffic (billions of long ton-miles)					
Road	50.4	51.9	9.0	8.3	10.5
Rail	14.9	41.4	4.7	0.9	10.9
Inland water	0.1	28.8	4.2	5.7	—
Coastal ships	13.1	—	—	—	3.8
Total	78.5	122.1	17.9	14.9	25.2

Source: Organization of Economic Co-operation and Development, *Economic Surveys: Belgium, Luxembourg Economic Union* (July 1973); Hammond's *World Atlas*; International Road Union, *World Transport Data* (1973); Luxembourg, Office Statistique des Communautés Européennes, *Transports: Statistique Annuelle 1971*.

rate of entry is substantially greater in Belgium than it is in any other country except Great Britain. Even though unlimited nationwide licenses do have a market value, the market value is not high compared with the market value of licenses in West Germany. For the most part the market value of licenses reflects the cost of waiting nine years. The revenue required to qualify for a national license—40,000 Belgian francs per ton of capacity—is not onerous, especially since in recent times inflation has eroded the value of the Belgian franc. (Swedish statistics, for example, indicate that the average Swedish truck earned a great deal more than the equivalent of 40,000 Belgian francs per ton of capacity.) Bracket rates within Belgium apply only to international shipments and coal and steel movements, and these controls are not stringently enforced.

Table C–2
INTERNATIONAL COMPARISONS FOR THE SELECTED STATISTICS ON THE TRUCKING INDUSTRIES OF FIVE EUROPEAN COUNTRIES

Item	Great Britain	West Germany	Bel- gium	The Nether- lands	Sweden
New firms as percentage of number of firms	11.4[a]	0	5.6[b]	0.4	1.4[c]
Own-account trucking tons as percentage of total trucking tons	53	59	62	32	33
Percentage of empty miles of trucks					
Professional	34	45	34	46	33
Own-account	30	66	—	41	30
Profit as percentage of revenue	11.3	8.9	less than 10	4.2–8.3	1.2
Average bankruptcy rate (percent)	0.9	2.1	less than 0.3	0.3	0.6
Minimum optimum size of firms (number of vehicles)[d]	31–50	4–6	11–15	5–3	6–10

[a] Average rate of entry in each licensing area; includes firms expanding into new areas.

[b] Number of firms with new twenty-five-kilometer certificates as a percentage of all firms (twenty-five-kilometer and unlimited).

[c] Net increase in number of new firms during the last four years.

[d] Estimated using the "survivor technique." The "survivor technique" hypothesizes that firms of the most efficient size survive and firms of inefficient size either disappear or change to an efficient size. Firms are classified into size categories for two or more periods, and the smallest size category that shows a growth in number of firms is the minimum optimum size of firms. The figures for Great Britain were estimated using firms categorized by number of employees rather than by number of vehicles. Then, using a rough measure of the relationship between number of vehicles and number of employees, the estimates were translated into number of vehicles.

Source: Data compiled from tables for individual countries (see above). For percentage of empty miles, data was compiled from the following sources: Great Britain, Department of the Environment, "Survey of the Transport of Goods by Road, 1967–1968" (1971); West Germany, Bundesanstalt für den Güterfernverkehr; Belgium, Ministère des Communications et des Postes, Télégraphes et Téléphones, *Echos des Communications,* no. 3 (1971); Netherlands, Centraal Bureau voor de Statistiek, *Statistiek van het Binnenlands Goederenvervoer 1971* (The Hague: Staatsuitgeverij, 1972); Sweden, National Central Bureau of Statistics, *Statistical Reports,* NrT 1973:33.

Sweden made considerable progress toward free entry, though entry controls have been tightened again in the last two years. For freight forwarders in regular service, it has always been difficult to secure a new license. Swedish law prohibits licensed truckers from operating anywhere except within their own county or to and from their own county. This does impose some inefficiencies on the trucking industry, but because most traffic is local and because on long-haul trips a trucker would normally prefer a return load rather than a load to a different area, the restriction is not burdensome.

Ordinary road haulage in the Netherlands is free to a considerable extent. For existing firms there is substantial freedom to expand capacity, although it is difficult for a new firm to secure a license. In fact, the number of new firms as a percentage of all licensed firms is lower in the Netherlands than in any other European country studied except West Germany. Entry into regular-route scheduled service and into pickup and delivery service is quite restricted. Maximum rate controls exist but not controls on the minimum.

Britain and West Germany make an especially interesting contrast, while Belgium and the Netherlands are sufficiently alike except for their regulatory system to make an interesting comparison. Sweden would appear to be unique, although some insights can be gleaned from its experience.

In spite of the lack of direct measures of efficiency, some facts and figures are revealing. First, it is quite clear to even a casual observer that the West German economy is considerably more efficient than the British economy, while the Dutch economy appears to be slightly more efficient than the Belgian. The greater efficiency of the West Germans holds for the trucking industry as well. The West German parcels company that I visited appeared to be more efficient and to provide better service than the British parcels company I visited. The West Germans guaranteed delivery throughout the country in twenty-four to forty-eight hours; the British firm attempted to provide forty-eight to ninety-six hour service, but 25 percent of the shipments took more than ninety-six hours and some took as long as a week.

One illustrative example might make the point. The German firm reported that they had expanded in the last few years to handle international traffic. They approached one of their large domestic customers to solicit the customer's international business. The customer agreed to ship by them, on the condition that they provide as good service internationally as they were offering domestically. As a test, the customer asked the trucker to have an item weighing about thirty pounds picked up in Great Britain the next day and delivered the following day in West Germany. The trucker promised to do so. Later he called his British partner to explain the importance of this order. The next day when the regularly scheduled truck arrived from London, the item was not on it. The German trucker called his British partner again to ask what had happened. The British partner explained that the part had not arrived at his depot until 6:00 p.m. when his loaders were leaving for the night. The German asked why he had not put it on the truck himself. His partner replied: "What? Me put it on the truck?" [1]

This example reflects a pervasive British attitude toward work. Such examples could be multiplied endlessly both for the trucking industry and for the rest of the economy. They go far toward explaining the poor performance of the British economy since World War II. They also indicate why the West German economy is so much more efficient than the British.

Nevertheless, statistics provided by the West German regulatory commission show that in 1970 trucks were empty on 45 percent of the miles driven by professional truckers and 66 percent of those driven on own-account (see Table C–2). In Great Britain the comparable figures for 1967–68 were 34 and 30 percent. It is revealing that in 1972 Dutch professional trucks were empty for 46 percent of the miles driven, but Belgian professional vehicles were empty for only 34 percent. In other words, professional truckers in the least regulated countries managed to be filled for about two-thirds of the miles while in the more regulated countries the percentage was noticeably lower.

Many factors besides regulation affect the ability of truckers to secure backhauls and prevent empty mileage. If there is a significant imbalance in demand from one region to another and if rates are not allowed to reflect this imbalance, then there will be considerable empty mileage. In short-haul markets there is likely to be a larger percentage of empty mileage than in long-haul markets. Neither of these factors seems adequate to explain the differences noted. West German markets tend to be longer-haul than markets in any other country: the median long-haul (over 50 kilometers) freight shipment by all modes of transport in West Germany is 148 miles; the median in Great Britain is

---

[1] Interview with Helmut Frech of Spedition Frech, 5 December 1973.

63 miles, in Belgium 65 miles, in the Netherlands 71 miles, and in Sweden 79 miles. Unfortunately there are no data on the question, but it seems unlikely that imbalances in demand are greater in West Germany than in Britain. West Germany has a significant imbalance problem with areas near the border of East Germany and with West Berlin. But Britain has similar imbalance problems with Scotland, parts of Wales, and Cornwall. Most of British industry is located in the Midlands or London while West German industry is spread throughout the country in a much more even pattern.

Thus, notwithstanding the more efficient nature of the West German trucker, his industry in at least one important dimension is operating less efficiently than its British counterpart. The most likely explanation is that rate regulation has prevented the use of price competition to secure backhauls.

In the Netherlands it would seem that licensing has also had an adverse effect. The unfilled Dutch trucks are probably a result of the restrictions on the number of different shippers that an irregular-route carrier can handle in one shipment, the frequency requirements for regular-route carriers, and the artificial separation of the two segments of the industry. It should be noted that on the largest vehicles, large truck-trailers, the Dutch did manage to fill the professional trucks for 63 percent of the miles, while own-account trucks were filled 65 percent of the time. On the other hand, Belgian professional truckers using large truck-trailers managed to fill their vehicles for 80 percent of their miles.

Own-account trucks in Sweden, the Netherlands, and Great Britain managed to have a smaller percentage of miles empty than did professional truckers. (There is no figure for own-account truckers in Belgium.) But in West Germany own-account truckers did very poorly, being empty for 66 percent of the time. Some 59 percent of the ton-miles driven in Germany were performed by own-account vehicles, a figure only exceeded in Belgium where short distances make own-account trucking attractive. Thus West Germany shows the anomalous characteristic of having a relatively high level of own-account trucking, in spite of discriminatory taxes and efforts by government authorities to discourage it, coupled with the fact that own-account trucking is highly inefficient because of the large percentage of miles empty. This suggests that shippers find regulated West German professional trucking either to be expensive or to offer poor service—or both.

Table WG–4 on page 49 above lists the reasons that German firms gave for using their trucks. The first, fourth, fifth, and seventh reasons indicate that service quality is not all it might be. The third reason shows that freight rates are considered to be too high. Note that regulation is often justified on the grounds that it makes it possible for truckers to earn enough on major routes to offer service to remote areas. The seventh reason, poor service to remote areas, suggests that trucking firms are naturally unwilling to cross-subsidize unprofitable service from profitable operations. In none of the remaining countries studied were there any reports of difficulties in securing professional trucking service to remote areas. Even northern Scotland and northern Sweden seemed to be well served. We can conclude therefore that strict regulation leads to poorer service than is offered in a relatively free market.

Regulation also tends to inflate rates. Table C–3 shows the impact of regulation on rates. This table is based on figures of actual freight charges paid by one large manufacturing firm which distributes its products in each of the countries. As can be seen from the second line of the table, the rate per ton-mile in 1973 was over 50 percent higher in West Germany than it was in any other European country. A spokesman for the company said that in 1970–71 freight rates in West Germany were 25 percent above those in Great Britain. As was noted in Chapter 1, complete deregulation of British trucking in 1971 led to a reduction in rates. In West Germany, however, real rates have climbed.

In Chapter 2 it was estimated that the monopoly rents reflected in the value of West German licenses implied that rates were 11 percent higher than they would be otherwise. A direct comparison between rates in Germany and elsewhere suggests that the inflation in rates may be 50 percent or more. One explanation for the difference between these two estimates is that regulation has fostered inefficiencies resulting in higher costs. Thus the 11 percent higher rates that are monopoly gains may be superadded to higher costs resulting from regulation.

The large manufacturer whose rates are shown in Table C–3 also paid about 25 percent more per ton-mile for shipping goods into the Netherlands than in moving goods around Belgium. This does not merely reflect the strict regulatory system in the Netherlands. The figure for the Netherlands is actually for an international movement from Belgium, while all the other rates are for domestic shipments, and the higher rate may simply reflect the tariff bracket system imposed by the

Table C-3

COMPARISON OF FREIGHT RATES FOR ONE SHIPPER IN U.S. CENTS PER LONG TON FOR SAME PRODUCT
(per mile)

Item	Great Britain	West Germany	Belgium	Nether-lands	Sweden	U.S.
Miles shipped	180	217	(flat rate)	140	200	203
Rate (cents per ton)	6.0	10.1	4.5	5.7	5.0	9.8
Motor vehicle tax (32-ton vehicle)	$1,269.60	$2,726.40	$1,194.00	$2,287.20	$2,533.20	
Fuel tax (cents per U.S. gallon)	64.5	56.3	23.6	6.4	48.1	
Total taxes per year						
Assumption A	$4,632	$5,633	$2,412	$2,633	$5,033	
Assumption B	$4,022	$5,105	$2,191	$2,570	$4,577	
Estimated rate (cents per ton) if taxes are removed						
Assumption A	5.3	8.4	3.8	4.9	3.6	
Assumption B	5.2	8.3	3.7	4.8	3.4	

Note: Freight rates are for 1973, but taxes are for 1972 and may have changed. To compute taxes it is assumed that a loaded 32-ton vehicle gets 6.6 miles to the U.S. gallon. Taxes A assumes that vehicle travels 34,000 miles (55,000 kms) per year and Taxes B assumes vehicle travels 27,900 miles (45,000 kms) per year. To compute the tax per ton/mile, it was assumed that on average ten tons were carried in a 32-ton vehicle for each mile driven including empty hauls. This corresponds with about a 50 percent load factor and is consistent with Swedish, Belgian, and West German figures. Exchange rates used: $1 equals 2.5 DM, $2.40 equals 2.6 DG, $1 equals £1, $1 equals 40 BF, $1 equals 4.25 Kr.

Source: Most data compiled from a report of a major U.S. shipper. Data for taxes are from *Verkehrs-Wirtschaftliche Zahlen 1972* (Frankfurt: Bundesverband des Deutchen Güterfernverkehrs, 1973).

European Economic Community. Any Belgian trucker, as well as any irregular licensed Dutch trucker, could participate in such an international movement within the Benelux countries.

Spokesmen for German truckers claim that the high rates within West Germany are a result of the high taxes imposed on the industry.[2] In the second half of Table C–3 an attempt has been made to calculate the taxes paid on a thirty-two-ton vehicle each year for two different levels of usage. West German taxes are clearly much higher than taxes in most other countries, although taxes are substantial in Sweden and Great Britain. In the lower portion of the table an estimate is made for what freight rates would be without taxes. As can be seen, West German rates would still be considerably higher than rates in other countries. The lowest rates after taxes are removed are found in two of the three least regulated countries, Belgium and Sweden. England and the Netherlands charge median rates. A rather poor road system may explain the relatively high charges found in Great Britain.

Of course there are other factors that influence the level of tariffs. Labor costs are clearly important. Such costs are higher in West Germany than in Holland, but they are also substantial in Belgium and Sweden. It is hard to compare British labor costs with labor costs in other countries, although wage rates generally tend to be low in Britain. Part of the explanation for different rates could be labor costs, but it seems unlikely that the small differences between German labor costs and the costs in other countries having high labor costs could go far toward explaining the substantial differences in rates.

British rates also appear to be high in comparison with the rates in other countries (with the exception of West Germany). Since deregulation, however, these rates have been falling, and in time they may fall to the level of rates in Belgium. It is also possible that because of the national attitudes toward work and because of the inadequate road system, rates in England will stay relatively high.

High freight rates in West Germany do not seem to have generated profits that are high in comparison with those in other countries (see Table C–2). Apparently high rates are offset by low truck utilization to produce fairly normal rates of profit. It is apparent from these figures that regulation does not markedly improve profits. The highest

---

[2] Interview with Mr. Binbrook of the Bundesverband des Deutschen Güterfernverkehrs, Frankfurt, November 1973.

rate of profit on revenue was earned in the country with no economic regulation—Great Britain.

As mentioned in Chapter 5, the Swedish statistics appear to be a little odd. Accounting procedures and income tax conventions must explain the difference since within Sweden the profit rate in trucking is no lower than the rate for other highly competitive small-enterprise industries.

The statistics shown in Table C–2 indicate that the bankruptcy rate is high in Britain (nearly 1 percent) but that it is markedly higher in West Germany. These figures should be treated with caution since the ease of bankruptcy as well as its definition may differ significantly among countries. However, it is fair to conclude that regulation has not eliminated the risks of bankruptcy.

Regulation appears to have affected the size structure of firms. The largest firms, both private and government-owned, are found in Great Britain, mainly as a result of the nationalization of the trucking industry by the Labour government after World War II. This nationalization resulted in a very large government enterprise that is now called the National Freight Corporation. When the Conservatives denationalized the industry in the 1950s, they had considerable difficulty selling many of the vehicles so that the remaining national company is still quite large. The sale of vehicles at that time also encouraged the formation of large private companies.

Some private British companies have as many as 4,500 vehicles, but firms in other European countries are much smaller. Even in the United States no company owns more than 2,000 vehicles, although one company leases over 5,000 vehicles with drivers.[3] West Germany has a few companies with 500 to 700 vehicles; the largest in Belgium has about 400 vehicles; and in the Netherlands the largest private firm has approximately 300, although the state-owned company has more than 1,000. In Sweden the largest single private trucking enterprise has about 100 vehicles. Thus, even though the largest firms are found in the least regulated market, the European country with the next largest firms is West Germany—the most regulated country.

Simple concentration statistics would indicate that the trucking industry is most concentrated in Great Britain, but these statistics are

[3] Interstate Commerce Commission, *Transport Statistics in the United States Year Ended December 31, 1971,* pt. 7: *Motor Carriers,* release 2.

misleading. In West Germany and Sweden, for example, there are cooperative arrangements among firms that make statistics on the size of individual firms irrelevant. Subcontracting on a long-term basis is common in Belgium and used extensively in the Netherlands. Although the assertion cannot be documented, it seems probable that actual market concentration is lower in Great Britain than it is in any other country.

In all five European countries the size category including the largest firms (that is, firms with more than ten or twenty vehicles) has grown the most rapidly. As Table C-2 shows, the minimum size that is surviving and growing relative to the industry as a whole (often called the minimum optimum size) differs among the countries. The minimum optimum size in Great Britain is considerably larger than the minimum optimum size in any other European country, and the minimum optimum size is smallest in West Germany. Regulation (which ensures a profit by even the inefficient) and market cooperative arrangements (which mitigate some of the disabilities of small size) undoubtedly permit the existence of smaller firms than would exist otherwise. The minimum optimum size is larger in Belgium than in the Netherlands or Sweden. Regulation does appear to permit the survival of smaller firms. Conversely, a free market tends to foster larger firms. However, in a free market, such as Great Britain, a large number of firms of varying size coexist and compete, and there is no tendency toward monopoly.

Except for regulation in the Netherlands, part of the original motivation for regulation was a desire to protect the railroads from road competition. To a large extent it appears to have failed in that mission. In Great Britain, Belgium, and Sweden the governments acknowledged the failure and began deregulation. West Germany still maintains an active program to encourage rail freight traffic and this, coupled with regulation, has resulted in rail movement of some 34 percent of the ton-miles moved in West Germany. Regulation, by increasing rates and producing poorer service, may have contributed to the relatively large proportion of goods moving by rail. The high taxes on roads and the long transport distances involved in West Germany, however, have also played a part, and it is impossible to find out how much regulation has contributed to the relatively high proportion of goods moving by rail. Sweden, which has had a fairly free transport system in recent years, has the highest proportion of ton-miles moved by rail (43 percent) among all the European countries studied. This high proportion may be traced to the relatively few miles of roads in Sweden and the large distances over which goods must travel. The goods must move by rail when there is no alternative.

When government commissions examined the impact of regulation in Sweden and Great Britain they found that not only had regulation failed to protect the traffic of the railroads but it had tended to foster monopolies and produce inefficiencies. In West Germany the result had been similar: regulation has produced inefficiencies, has created monopolies, and has not contributed significantly to solution of the railroad problem. The West German Federal Railroad is losing money. If West Germany or other countries want to increase the proportion of goods moved by rail, high taxes on road haulage would be more efficient than regulation.

The other objective of transportation regulation has been to stabilize the transportation market and prevent excessive competition from resulting in "cut-throat" price-cutting. Countries with substantial barriers to entry know that there are many potential truckers. Existing truckers fear these new truckers would destabilize the market if they were allowed to operate. High rates protected by regulation do tend to attract potential entrants. But would the industry be destabilized if entry barriers were actually removed?

The experience in Sweden and Great Britain suggests that immediately after deregulation there would be a flurry of new entrants, but a few years later—it was two in Great Britain and about five in Sweden—the number of entrants would drop significantly. In neither the Swedish experience nor the experience in Great Britain is there any evidence that the market is destabilized by deregulation. Profits continue adequate to generate investment, and in Great Britain there has been no reduction in profits after deregulation. Freight rates do seem to have declined but increased efficiencies have preserved earnings. Rates tend to be stable and service quality good. There is no evidence whatsoever that deregulation would destabilize the trucking industry.

In sum, regulation reduces efficiency, increases rates, reduces service quality, and does not markedly improve profits. It tends to foster small firms of suboptimal size. It does not greatly benefit railroads and is unnecessary for stabilizing the trucking industry.

7
Lessons for the United States

Regulation of trucking in the United States was instituted in 1935. The railroads and the Interstate Commerce Commission which regulated the railroads were the major advocates of regulation, but there were in addition a number of large truckers who saw government control as a device for stabilizing the industry. The railroads wanted regulation because the trucking industry, by offering low rates and quick service, was siphoning off the most profitable rail traffic. Moreover, both the rail and the trucking industries were suffering from the effects of the Depression and viewed regulation as a means of improving profits.

The Motor Carrier Act of 1935 established a regulatory framework that has changed only slightly to this day. This act required all interstate common carrier trucking firms, with some specific exceptions, to have a certificate of public convenience and necessity issued by the Interstate Commerce Commission. The major exceptions were those firms hauling fish, livestock, or agricultural commodities (but not including any products manufactured from these). The law requires that the certificate

> specify the service to be rendered and the routes over which, the fixed termini, if any, between which, and the intermediate and off-route points, if any, and in case of operatives not over specified routes or between fixed termini, the territory within which, the motor carriers is authorized to operate. . . .[1]

The ICC, in issuing certificates of public convenience and necessity, has interpreted this mandate narrowly. The original ("grandfather") certificates were issued only for that business a trucker could prove he hauled and only between those points for which he could show he

---

[1] 49 U.S.C., Sec. 308(a).

operated. A study of the original certification process showed that 62 percent of the truckers were limited to special commodities and that 40 percent of those were limited to one commodity or commodity class.[2] Some 80 percent had been limited to six or fewer commodity classes. Some 70 percent of the regular route common carriers were not allowed full authority to serve intermediate points on their routes, and approximately 10 percent had no authority to serve any intermediate point; clearly, these restrictions do little to ensure the provision of service to smaller towns. The study also found that a third of the common carrier truckers had return-trip limitations, with almost 10 percent having no authority to haul goods on their return trip.

The law requires that all rates and fares be reasonable and not unjustly discriminatory. The ICC may suspend a rate for up to seven months, prescribe the maximum rate, the minimum rate, or the actual rate. In practice the ICC has been more interested in minimum than in maximum rates. Rates are set initially by rate bureaus, which with ICC approval are exempt from the antitrust laws. Carriers are permitted to file rates individually, but if the rate filed is below existing rates, the rate bureau usually protests and the rate, almost inevitably, is suspended. If the carrier seeking the lower rate wishes to pursue the matter, a lawyer skilled in administrative law will be needed to argue the case with the commission. Usually the carrier simply withdraws the proposed rate—and probably in most cases a carrier interested in offering a lower rate never bothers to file the proposal, knowing the futility of doing so.[3]

New entry into trucking is difficult. The commission acts on the principle that if existing carriers can provide the proposed service they should be given the opportunity to do so before a new carrier is certificated. The ICC asserted in a recent case that "it has consistently been held that existing carriers should be afforded the opportunity to transport all the traffic which they can handle adequately, economically, and efficiently in the territory they serve before a new service is authorized."[4] The ICC operates on the assumption that if one carrier is

---

[2] Board of Investigation and Research, *Federal Regulatory Restrictions upon Motor and Water Carriers*, 79th Congress, 1st sess., 1945, Senate document no. 78.
[3] See Thomas Gale Moore, *Freight Transportation Regulation* (Washington, D. C.: American Enterprise Institute, 1972), especially chap. 4, for a full discussion of these issues.
[4] 110 M.C.C. 180, 184-85.

able to offer service to a shipper, the shipper's desire for an alternative carrier is without merit. In fact the commission's policy appears to be designed to protect each of the approximately 15,000 ICC licensed truckers from additional competition.

New firms are usually given authority to carry specific commodities from one point to another provided that no other firm already has the authority to service that market. If an existing firm is authorized to serve the projected needs, the prospective entrant's request for a certificate of convenience and necessity will be denied.

In order to prevent competition from eroding the profits of existing licensed carriers, the commission normally will not approve changes in authorized routes for existing carriers if the change would allow the carrier to offer appreciably faster service. Because of the fuel shortage, the commission issued a rule in February 1974 that irregular-route carriers with circuity less than 20 percent could upon application secure authority to remove such circuity but those with circuity greater than 20 percent would, if they want to continue the service, have to go through the normal procedures to secure a certificate of convenience and necessity.[5] Before this ruling the ICC had used approximately 6 percent extra mileage required by truckers' certificates as the usual level of circuity in interstate trucking.[6] The figure was derived from a weighted average based on some old ICC traffic studies. Since carriers with large circuity suffer a competitive disadvantage and traffic with large circuity is not as profitable as traffic with more direct routing, not much tonnage could be expected on routes with a great deal of circuity. Nevertheless, if the 6 percent circuity were eliminated, costs could be reduced approximately 3 percent, since line-haul costs are about half of total costs for long-distance haulage.

Notwithstanding present energy concerns, the commission continues to consider maintenance of competitive relationships to be of paramount importance. For example, in February 1974, at a time of acute fuel shortages, the commission turned down a request by Consolidated Freightways Corp. for reducing the mileage between Minneap-

---

[5] 119 M.C.C. 530. The commission announced in February 1975 that it had received 20,000 applications to remove circuity and that those upon which it had acted favorably would save 300 million gallons of motor fuel annually.

[6] Interstate Commerce Commission, Bureau of Accounts, "Cost of Transporting Freight by Class I and Class II Motor Common Carriers of General Commodities, Performing Transcontinental Service, 1969," Statement No. 2 C14-69 (Washington, D. C., August 1971), p. 6.

olis-St. Paul, Minnesota and Dallas, Texas and Oklahoma from 1,401 miles to 1,024 miles, a saving of 377 miles and elimination of a circuity of 37 percent. Consolidated Freightways argued that the shorter distance would reduce transit time 8.5 hours, while the four competitors protesting the request argued that the saving was likely to be as much as 10.5 hours. The commission ruled that such an authorization would save Consolidated one day in transit and thus change the competitive structure. The commission therefore denied the request.[7]

Private carriage is exempt from regulation but not unaffected by it. Regulation bars the trucks of a wholly-owned subsidiary from carrying goods for the parent corporation or for any other subsidiary of the company. It also bars the trucks from hauling for compensation any goods except exempt agricultural commodities and restricts the leasing of private trucks to certificated carriers. These restrictions make private trucking more expensive than it would be were trucking not regulated.

Contract carriage also is regulated in the United States. Contract carriers need permits issued by the ICC and their rates—like those of common carriers—are subject to control. Contract carrier rates are lower than common carrier rates. It would appear to be as difficult to receive a permit for contract carriage as for common carriage.[8] Contract carriers are also limited in the number of customers they may serve.

The Effects of Regulation

The original objective of regulation, at least the objective of the railroads in urging regulation, was to prevent the diversion of rail traffic to the roads and thus to improve the railroad profit position. As can be seen from Table U.S.–1, regulation has not prevented the diversion of traffic from railroads to motor carriers. The growth in the motor vehicle share of the market is virtually mirrored by the loss of market share held by railroads, with barge lines and ships on the Great Lakes maintaining a constant 20 percent of the market.

Table U.S.–2 shows that regulation has not prevented a marked decline in the profits of major railroads. This does not mean, of course, that regulation either caused the decline or had no effect on profits.

---

[7] Files of the Interstate Commerce Commission Motor Carrier Division.

[8] See Moore, *Freight Transportation Regulation,* chap. 4.

Table U.S.–1

FREIGHT TRANSPORTED BY RAILROADS, MOTOR VEHICLES, INLAND WATERWAYS, SELECTED YEARS, 1940–74

Year	Railroads		Motor Vehicles		Inland Waterways	
	Billions of ton-miles	Percentage of total	Billions of ton-miles	Percentage of total	Billions of ton-miles	Percentage of total
1940	412	70	62	10	118	20
1945	736	78	67	7	143	15
1950	628	65	173	18	163	17
1955	655	60	223	20	217	20
1960	595	54	285	26	220	20
1965	721	54	359	27	262	20
1970	771	51	412	27	319	21
1974[a]	861	50	510	30	347	20

[a] Preliminary.

Source: *Statistical Abstract of the United States, 1973* (Washington, D. C.: U.S. Bureau of the Census, 1973), table 4; George Hilton, *Northeast Railroad Problem* (Washington, D. C.: American Enterprise Institute, 1975), p. 54.

It is quite possible that without regulation of trucking, railroad earnings would be even smaller than they are. It is also possible that without regulation of either trucking or railroads they would be higher.

Regulation has resulted in higher freight rates than would otherwise be in effect. In the middle 1950s a series of court decisions held that fresh dressed poultry (1955), frozen poultry (1956), and frozen fruits and vegetables (1956) were all exempt commodities under the ICC act and therefore free from regulation. The Department of Agriculture studied what happened to rates after deregulation and found that rates on fresh poultry fell from 12 to 53 percent depending on the particular market and rates on frozen poultry fell 15 to 59 percent. The unweighted average decline in rates was 33 percent for fresh poultry and 36 percent for frozen. Moreover charges for extra stop-offs were either reduced or eliminated and the number of permitted stops increased. The weighted average decline in rates for hauling frozen fruits and vegetables was 19 percent over a period of time when rail rates on

Table U.S.–2

RAILROAD PROFITS AND PROFIT RATES, SELECTED YEARS, 1929–74

Year	Net Railroad Operating Income ($ million)	Rate of Return on Average Net Investment (percent)
1929	1,251.7	5.30
1944	1,106.3	4.70
1951	942.5	3.76
1955	1,128.0	4.22
1963	805.7	3.12
1964	818.2	3.16
1965	961.5	3.69
1966	1,045.9	3.90
1967	676.4	2.46
1968	677.6	2.44
1969	654.7	2.36
1970	485.9	1.73
1971	695.5	2.47
1972	827.7	2.97
1973	849.3	3.05
1974	981.4	3.45

Source: Data from the Association of American Railroads: *Statistics of the Railroads of Class I in the United States* (August 1974) and *Yearbook of Railroad Facts, 1975.*

the same commodities were going up 6 to 14 percent.[9] In summarizing these studies the Department of Agriculture concluded that

> Not only are the kinds of services offered expanded, but the quality of service improves also. In-transit time for motor carriers is reduced, sometimes by half. Schedules and routes are made to suit the shipper. Increased competition causes

[9] J. R. Snitzler and R. J. Byrne, *Interstate Trucking of Fresh and Frozen Poultry under Agricultural Exemption*, Marketing Research Report No. 224 (Washington, D. C.: U.S. Department of Agriculture, 1958), and Snitzler and Byrne, *Interstate Trucking of Frozen Fruits and Vegetables under Agricultural Exemption*, Marketing Research Report No. 315 (Washington, D. C.: U.S. Department of Agriculture, 1959).

the carriers to be more eager to please and resolute to maintain good service.[10]

James Sloss compared trucking in unregulated provinces of Canada with trucking in regulated provinces and in the United States and found that revenues per ton-mile of unregulated trucking were 6.73 percent lower than the revenues per ton-mile in the regulated areas. For two reasons the 6.73 percent comparison may understate the magnitude of the difference in rates. First, Sloss lumped all "regulated" provinces in Canada with the United States. Regulation is considerably more comprehensive in the United States than in any province of Canada. In fact, one of his "regulated" provinces—British Columbia—does not, according to extraprovincial carriers, regulate rates. On the other hand, several provinces in the "unregulated" area do require the publication of rates and adherence to them, so that much of the "unregulated" sector is controlled in some way.[11] Moreover, if regulation raised rates an average of 20 percent, those rates that went up the most would be expected on average to lead to the greatest reduction in traffic. As a consequence revenues per ton-mile would be expected to rise by much less than 20 percent.

Chapter 6 reports on rates furnished by one large firm which ships the same commodities in each of the countries considered. This company was kind enough to furnish similar data for the United States on a confidential basis. The West German rates are comparable with the rates in the United States. The rates in the more competitive countries are an average 43 percent lower than the rates in the United States.[12] This of course may result from other factors besides regulation, although presumably regulating accounts for at least part of the difference. It must be admitted that wages for U.S. truck drivers are higher than the wages paid in Europe but fuel costs are lower in the United States than abroad. Labor compensation does account for about 47 percent of all

---

[10] U.S., Congress, House, Committee on Interstate and Foreign Commerce, *Synopses of U.S. Department of Agriculture Marketing Research Reports Comparing Rates and Services under Regulation and Deregulation, Hearings,* before the Subcommittee on Transportation and Aeronautics, on the Transportation Act of 1972, 92d Cong., 2d sess., 1972, pt. 1, p. 155.

[11] James Sloss, "Regulation of Motor Freight Transportation: A Quantitative Evaluation of Policy," *The Bell Journal of Economics and Management Science,* vol. 1, no. 2 (Autumn 1970), pp. 327-66.

[12] See Table C-1, p. 123 above.

Table U.S.–3
U.S. COMMON CARRIER TRUCKING PROFIT RATES, 1971

	Total Profits ($ million)	Profits as Percentage of Revenue	Profits as Percentage of Total Assets
10 largest carriers	167.93	7.1	18.6
All class I	772.5	5.9	13.6
Class II	46.1	3.7	7.8
Class I and II	818.6	5.7	13.1

Source: Interstate Commerce Commission, *Transport Statistics in the United States Year Ended December 31, 1971*, pt. 7: *Motor Carriers*, release 2.

costs in the United States.[13] In contrast, total personnel costs are about 35 percent of all costs in West German long-distance professional trucking. In England, however, wages constitute over half of the total expenses of professional truckers. The extent to which rates in the United States are higher than abroad because of higher wages cannot be ascertained, but it seems unlikely that wage differentials alone could explain the disparities.

The National Broiler Council has produced some interesting data on what might happen to rates if the carriage of broilers was subject to regulation. It compared the regulated rates for carrying cooked poultry with the unregulated rates for fresh dressed poultry (a similar product) and found that the regulated rates for the same distances, same routes, and same weights were on average 48.3 percent higher than the unregulated rates. The greater the distance, the larger the percentage increase of regulated over unregulated rates.[14]

As Table U.S.–3 shows, higher rates do not seem to have contributed significantly to reported profits. The operating ratio for ICC-regulated truckers (operating costs as a percentage of revenue) is about 94 percent,[15] while the average return before taxes on assets for all

[13] Interstate Commerce Commission, *Transport Statistics in the United States Year Ended December 31, 1971*, pt. 7, *Motor Carriers*, release 2.

[14] U.S., Congress, House, Committee on Interstate and Foreign Commerce, *Statement of the National Broiler Council, Hearings,* before the Subcommittee on Transportation and Aeronautics, on the Transportation Act of 1972, 92d Cong., 2d sess., 1972, p. 1434.

[15] Interstate Commerce Commission, *Transport Statistics 1971*, pt. 7.

carriers was only 13.1 percent. On the other hand for the ten largest carriers net operating revenue as a percentage of total assets was 18.6 percent in 1971.[16] Even this figure is not an especially high pretax rate of profits.

The profit figures may be misleading. Whenever a firm is purchased, the cost of the acquisition is added to the assets. Thus part of any monopoly rents become capitalized into the asset value of the firm. In addition, smaller firms often pay their owner-operators large salaries and put wives and children on the payroll so that the firm will not appear to regulators to be extraordinarily profitable. Notwithstanding these factors the industry does not appear to be as profitable as the inflated freight rates would suggest.

As I have suggested elsewhere, the reason that profits are not raised by regulation is that regulation raises costs.[17] Trucks are forced to go miles out of their way to deliver goods because of route and gateway restrictions in their certificates. Backhaul restrictions and restrictions on commodities that can be carried add to costs and inefficiency. Nonprice competition among carriers fosters extra costs for firms and dissipates the monopoly profits.

Service quality by regulated carriers seems to be less than optimum. Over the years shippers have complained about the unwillingness of carriers to truck small loads to out-of-the-way communities. In 1970 the ICC held hearings on this subject at which forty-four groups of shippers, shipper associations, and others complained about service quality; only groups representing carriers supported existing service levels.[18] Most of the complaints involved the reluctance of licensed common carriers to serve authorized points.

On the other hand, farmers, farm cooperatives, and others making use of *unregulated* agricultural carriers do not complain about the service they get. By their very nature farm trucks have to serve small communities and out-of-the-way places with less-than-truck-load lots. Yet shippers have no trouble getting such service from these unregulated carriers. For example, the National Broiler Council, when testifying against bringing the trucking of broilers under regulation, stated: "The necessity of having available carriers with flexibility in serving a variety of destinations is vital to agricultural industries where perishable prod-

---

[16] Ibid.

[17] Moore, *Freight Transportation Regulation*.

[18] 111 M.C.C. 427.

Table U.S.–4

RATING OF REGULATED AND NONREGULATED MOTOR CARRIERS
(percent)

	Nonregulated Carriers Are—		
Characteristic	Better than regulated	Equal to regulated	Less satisfactory than regulated
Quality of trucks	13	84	3
Promptness of delivery service	58	39	3
Availability of trucks	65	30	5
Reliability	51	47	2
Adjustment of claims	47	53	0
Need for supervision	31	69	0
Willingness to serve off-line points	69	27	3

Note: These figures are percent of membership of National Broiler Council who answered their survey about regulated and unregulated motor carriers.

Source: U.S., Congress, House, Committee on Interstate and Foreign Commerce, *Statement of the National Broiler Council, Hearings,* before the Subcommittee on Transportation and Aeronautics, on the Transportation Act of 1972, 92d Cong., 2d sess., 1972, p. 1433.

ucts must be moved from producing areas to consumption centers efficiently if they are to retain their market value." [19]

The council reported on a survey conducted among its members on their experience with regulated and unregulated carriers. Table U.S.–4 reproduces the findings of the survey. In each of seven respects more shippers found that the quality of unregulated trucking was better than found the quality of regulated trucking better.

These results are strikingly similar to the findings of a 1959 Department of Agriculture study of service quality for the products that had become deregulated through court decisions.[20] This study asked 107 processors of frozen food items the advantages and disadvantages of regulated and unregulated carriage. Forty-one of the processors com-

[19] *Statement of the National Broiler Council, Hearings,* Transportation Act of 1972, p. 1433.

[20] U.S. Department of Agriculture, *Interstate Trucking of Frozen Fruits and Vegetables.*

plained about the unwillingness of regulated carriers to haul less-than-truck-load shipments or to serve off-line points. No processor cited this as a problem with unregulated carriers. In general the processors found more to praise than to condemn in unregulated carriage and more to condemn and less to praise in regulated carriage.

ICC regulations have imposed a great many inefficiencies on the industry. Trucks must drive extra miles, traffic cannot be picked up at all points, licenses restrict the commodities that can be handled, authority to carry on the backhaul may be missing. As I have argued elsewhere, these restrictions, along with nonprice competition and the sheltered market position of firms, have resulted in considerable waste.[21] From the data cited above it would appear that rates would be at least 20 percent lower without regulation, while profits under regulation do not seem to be particularly high. I have estimated that the waste generated in common carrier trucking from regulation in 1968 was between $1.4 billion and $1.9 billion.[22] With inflation the current loss may easily exceed $2 billion. Moreover, regulation prevents firms hauling on own-account from soliciting traffic on the backhaul and consequently those vehicles travel empty or partly empty more of the time than would be necessary without regulation. Exempt carriers of agricultural commodities are limited on the amount of backhaul traffic they can solicit to 15 percent of their total business, which forces them to run many empty miles and causes unnecessary consumption of motor fuel.

Lessons

Regulation appears to have the same general impact wherever it is imposed. Where there is strict regulation, such as in West Germany and the United States, rates are higher—about 40 to 50 percent in both cases—than the rates charged in nonregulated sectors or in nonregulated economies. Regulation does not produce better service to small communities; judging from complaints, it produces worse service. In West Germany shippers expressed some complaints about lack of service to out-of-the-way places. The relatively high percentage of goods carried

---

[21] Thomas Gale Moore, "Deregulating Surface Freight Transportation," in *Promoting Competition in Regulated Markets,* A. Phillips, ed. (Washington, D. C.: Brookings Institution, 1975).

[22] Ibid.

145

by private truck in long-distance hauls in West Germany also indicates shipper dissatisfaction with professional carriers. On the other hand, in England, Belgium, and Sweden—the three unregulated states—no complaints by shippers were detected. In the United States the evidence supports the proposition that unregulated agricultural carriers offer better service than regulated common carriers.

Great Britain is the only country in this study that has completely deregulated, although Belgium and Sweden have gone very far toward deregulation. Several lessons can be drawn from the experience these countries have had with deregulation. It appears that deregulation leads to a contraction in private carriage and an expansion in professional carriage. Faced with lower rates and better service, shippers give up hauling for themselves and turn to specialized truckers.

Just as rates declined in England after deregulation, they would decline in the United States. Because rates here are held at much higher levels than they were in Great Britain, the reduction in U.S. rates would probably be sharper. Much care, therefore, is necessary in fashioning a deregulation program. A deregulation scenario might take several years and start with provisions for freely varying rates within fixed limits, then gradually expand the bands. The West German experience indicates that most rates would tend to hug the bottom of a given band. Eventually, however, the lower limit of the band would go below the competitive rate and rates would then be negotiated freely.

To prevent the very rapid influx of new trucking firms that occurred in both Great Britain and Sweden, entry restrictions should be relaxed slowly. But the British experience indicates that after the transition is made the industry would be completely stable. Because most shippers are concerned with quality of service as well as with rates, they are reluctant to deal with unknown trucking firms. Therefore entry requires more than the simple purchase of a truck and the leasing of a terminal. It also requires the trucker to convince some shippers that he can offer good service at lower rates than existing carriers. Many shippers will want to deal only with experienced and known firms, and a new trucking firm will not be able to compete simply by offering discount rates.

In a completely unregulated environment there would be no legal barriers to entry, but new firms would encounter economic barriers. New firms did enter the industry in Great Britain (and would here also), but their entry did not lead to a sharp drop in rates. Freight rates in the

British Isles did not fall after deregulation in nominal terms but only after inflation was taken into account (that is, only in real terms). Actual agreements had considerable stability over time.

The English experience shows that profits in general would not be significantly hurt by deregulation. Some firms would clearly lose and others might gain in terms of a better route structure and a better balance of goods. It must be admitted, however, that British regulation was never as stringent as the U.S. regulatory structure, so the British profit experience may not be the pattern followed here.

The data indicate that there are economies of scale for firms up to the size of thirty-one to fifty vehicles. Larger firms do not have any advantage over medium-size firms, however, and small one-truck firms, offering specialized services, do exist and will continue to exist in Great Britain and in any unregulated market. There is no possibility of monopoly in trucking even though the number of firms offering to serve any one particular shipper at a particular point in time may not be large. A shipper dissatisfied with the rates or services offered could easily find a trucker serving other firms that would happily take on his business. Thus the number of potential competitors in each market is virtually unlimited.

After a transition period, complete deregulation would result in a stable, competitive industry offering better service than exists now at lower rates. Only the transition needs careful preparation and concern.

Both from an economic point of view and from a political point of view no serious effort should be made to move immediately to total deregulation, although that is the preferable long-run state. A useful first step therefore would be to require the ICC to establish margins within which rates could not be challenged. In addition the law should be changed to require the issuance of a certificate of public convenience and necessity whenever an applicant is fit, willing, and able and can show that shippers wish to use his services. For a transitional period, only existing certificate holders would be granted new certificates under this provision. No consideration should be given to the protests of other carriers. The ICC's authority to immunize collective rate making from the antitrust laws should be abolished. These steps will result in a significant reduction in regulation and a large increase in competitive freedom. Rates can be expected to fall to the floor of the bracket. Efficiency will be improved as existing carriers rationalize their routes and the products handled.

After experience is gained with partial deregulation, rate brackets can be widened. Finally all controls over rates would be removed and then, after another transitional period, the remaining requirements for a certificate of public convenience and necessity would be abolished. Deregulation would then be complete.

Conclusion

Regulation of motor carriers in the United States has not succeeded in protecting the market position of the railroads. What it has done is to create monopolies and oligopolies in particular transport markets, with the result that rates have been greatly inflated. These inflated rates, rather than leading to highly profitable firms, have been dissipated in inefficiencies so that costs are higher and profits not much greater than those found in nonregulated sectors of the economy. Moreover, it would appear that regulation has reduced the quality of the service provided by the trucking industry, especially to smaller cities and small towns.

A nonregulated trucking industry not only is theoretically preferable to regulation but in actual practice operates efficiently and in the public interest. This study has demonstrated that regulation is unnecessary as well as being undesirable.